Dad Differently

*An Emotional Guide to Pregnancy and Birth
for the Modern Father-to-Be*

Dad Differently
Book 1

Adam Fletcher

Wanderlust Words

Why This Book Exists

If you're reading this, it's likely two monumental things have happened in your life:

1. You've impregnated your lady-woman-wife-partner-person.
2. A friend or confused enemy gave you this book as a gift.

Three years ago, I was also a father-to-be. My days passed in an anxious fog. I was a mess of contradictions. I wanted to nest. I wanted to run away to Siberia and rustle elk. I wanted to research everything. I wanted to forget it was happening.

To help me through this difficult period, friends bought me fatherhood books with titles like *Super-Father-Heroman*.

In each, fatherhood was presented as a series of hackable challenges, often in checklist form. Depending on the metaphor of the moment, the baby was a finicky second-hand car whose quirks I had to master, a ticking bomb I had to heroically disarm, or an Ikea bookcase to assemble with my bare hands.

Logistics. Fatherhood was all logistics.

But it wasn't logistics keeping me up at night. I had YouTube tutorials to teach me brilliant diaper-folding hacks and how to install car seats. No, I was struggling with the inside, hard-to-reach parts of becoming a father: thoughts, feelings, fears, and emotions.

I never found a book that helped with that, so I promised myself that once my daughter turned two and I had more time, I'd write the one I'd needed.

This is that book.

I hope it helps you.

Adam

PS While my goal isn't to exclude anyone, this book focuses on heterosexual parenting couples, as that's the constellation I know. More should be written about other family and parenting constellations, but I'm not the person to write it. You'll also notice a bias towards couples expecting their first child because that's when you're most likely to receive these books, and when anxiety and excitement are highest.

PPS It was actually very expensive IVF science that impregnated my partner, Evelyn, along with my sperm (I presume—I didn't, like, check or anything, and I wasn't in the room at the time). Why am I telling you this? There's still some stigma around IVF. For some unfathomable reason, people really don't like to talk about it. As if it were a moral issue, rather than simply a bodily one. Personally, I think nothing good comes from not talking about things. I'm going to talk about everything. Especially birth. In excruciating detail. You're welcome.

Part One
The First Trimester
Narrowing the Divide

Trust

When she presented you with that pee-splashed stick—and those unbelievable, destiny-swerving double lines—the breath caught in your throat, didn't it?

Time seemed to both slow down and speed up.

"Me?" you said to yourself. "A *father*? But... I'm an idiot man-child. There are seven different stains on my trousers, five of which I can't identify. I consider a day in which I don't break a bone or accidentally set something on fire an enormous success. I can't care for a human. A whole human."

You looked at the face of your partner, the person you love most in the world, and were bowled over by the precariousness of everything, weren't you? All that could go wrong. All you could lose. Everything seemed both miraculous and desperately fragile.

In fact, it's fair to say you freaked the flip out, right?

Thanks for being honest about that.

We're all friends here. We can talk about this stuff. And anyway, panic is nothing to be ashamed of. Panic is just excess concern sprayed around indiscriminately—hysteria's cheap champagne.

You don't need to panic, buddy. Because what feels like a miracle—what will be the most monumental, memorable experience of your life—is actually, for our wider species, merely the most extraordinarily, exquisitely, devastatingly mundane development. The banalest of all banalities.

Another human for the pile. *Yay.*

Consider this. For you to exist, all of your ancestors, those sad, crusty, ancient losers who lived on lentils and wallpaper paste, had to be cool enough and resource-rich enough that they got laid often enough, had children regularly enough, and provided food and care punctually enough that those children became adults who made children who made more children who made more children who made more children who made more children who made more children who made more children in a perfect unbroken streak of fertility that stretches all the way back to organisms with scales, breathing through gills.

If we found it difficult to make other humans and keep them alive long enough to make other humans, there wouldn't be eight billion of us.

EIGHT BILLION.

Nothing is as precarious as it seems. For now, you just have to trust humans and their extraordinary fertility. Trust her body, which knows how to do this. Trust the hospitals, midwives, doctors, doulas, and gynaecologists who monitor, supervise, and educate, and who then deliver this tiny person, merely number eight billion and change for us but everything to you.

Trust that with ancient instincts, modern medical professionals, and a tribe of loving family and friends, you'll have way more help than you need.

Don't panic, buddy.

Trust. (Oh, and go wash your trousers.)

Futile Gestures

"You want a beer?" Evelyn asked, standing at the open fridge hunting for any high-calorie snack she hadn't already devoured. In the first trimester, Evelyn appeared to be in an eating contest with herself, sponsored by Snickers.

"I've given it up," I said, from the kitchen table.

"For, like, Lent?"

"No. For pregnancy."

She shut the fridge door. "Why would you do that?"

"The gesture?" I said, having expected praise. Where was my praise?

"It's nice," she said, crossing the kitchen to pat me on the hand. "But what's the point of more suffering? What do we gain from that?"

"Err... well... I mean, you'd give up alcohol for me if it was the other way round, right?"

She laughed for a long time. Cackled, actually.

"It's really the least I can do," I said. "We're a team. We're pregnant."

She went cross-eyed, so I went cross-eyed too, because maybe it was a pregnancy thing, and we did pregnancy things together. We were a team, in it to the bitter (blurry) end.

"Do you feel like you're on a bumpy ship?" she asked. "Do you have pregnancy diarrhoea? Is your vagina on fire?"

"Err… not so much, I suppose, no?"

"Yeah, because you aren't pregnant. So don't say 'we're pregnant'. And don't give up alcohol."

"I will," I said, my chin high and proud. "I'm a Modern Man. An ally."

"Let's see," she said, and I said nothing, because there's not much you can say to

"Let's see" other than "Uh-huh, yeah we will, you just wait."

Four days later, I walked into the living room carrying two glasses. She was on the couch, where she now lived and from where she liked to shout her various discontents at me, as if she were the star of a well-upholstered misery opera. She'd been too sick to go to work.

"What's that?" she asked, nodding at the other glass.

"A dark and stormy—oh," I said, and went cross-eyed again, for real this time. I had forgotten my valiant, brave, stupid, pointless pledge.

"And what's that?" she asked, gesturing to the glass in my right hand.

I lowered my head. "Your dark and stormy," I mumbled. "I've forgotten you're pregnant again, haven't I?"

"Yes."

"You'd think since it took us two years and thousands and thousands of euros, it would be monumental enough that I wouldn't forget it five times a day, right?"

She nodded. Slowly. "Yes."

"Do you ever forget?"

"All the time. Now give mine here so I can sniff it."

What Happens When Again?

I know that I said this book would be about warm, mushy feelings, not cold, rigid facts, but when it comes to closing the Divide, and accepting that there really is a future child growing in there, it can help to know a little of what's happening, when.

First trimester: stormy with a high chance of vomit

Mother: The first few weeks are usually a great time for both mother and father, full of optimism, novelty, and something akin to love's first flush—you're going to become a family!

However, those highs may be laced with fear and furious research. And, as the weeks pass, she may experience a rough physical ride. This is generally the bumpiest trimester.

She can expect morning sickness, which peaks at around week nine or ten, when levels of the pregnancy hormone human chorionic gonadotropin (hCG) are highest. When the body is flooded with hormones such as oestrogen and progesterone, there will be high highs, low lows, and deep retching over the toilet bowl. Despite being called "morning sickness," the nausea and vomiting can occur at any time of the day and will probably last for several weeks.

The surge in hormones, especially progesterone, can also lead to extreme tiredness. Increased blood flow and hormonal changes can cause sore, sensitive breasts. Many women experience SuperSmell (which can trigger nausea and passionate food aversions—more on that later).

At this point, your partner's body is working hard to support the foetus's growth and development, which can leave her feeling drained and needing both more rest and more support from you. In general, it's as if her body has a new job but doesn't know how to do it—yet. Your job is to be responsible for running the home and providing whatever care she needs while she's going through this really weird, intense, intimate experience of sharing her body with another human. It's like nothing you will ever know, and maybe beyond anyone's ability to fully describe.

Patience, understanding, and empathy are key.

Baby: By the fourth week of pregnancy, the fertilised egg has implanted in the uterus lining. The cells are dividing rapidly as the blastocyst becomes the less-exciting-sounding embryo, which grows to the impressive size of an entire poppy seed.

By week five, the heart is beating and the brain, the spinal cord, and the circulatory system begin development. By week seven, there are tiny arm and leg buds. Facial features start to form too, sort of, including primitive eyes, nose, and mouth.

By week nine, the embryo is officially a foetus, and all the major body systems are in place, if not online. It can move its limbs and has reflexes, such as sucking and swallowing.

Around week ten, the vital organs, including the kidneys and liver, are all functioning. Fingernails and hair follicles form. Yes, I said fingernails. The foetus is about the size of a strawberry.

By the time you've made it to the end of the first trimester, the heartbeat will be audible, facial features will be recognisable, and limbs will be fully formed, if not quite basketball ready. The placenta will be ready to take over the production of the hormones during the second and third trimesters, and this should help stabilise things for your partner. You'll be one-third of the way there. *Hurrah.*

The Divide

There was that initial high, those few nights of bad sleep, those few days of furious soul-searching, but now things are slipping back towards normalcy.

Life settles down again quickly.

Not so much for her, of course. As mentioned, she's probably having quite a rough physical ride, the poor bugger. There's more work for you to do around the house, but otherwise, that's pretty much it for the first trimester.

She probably doesn't need very much.

Which is a shame, almost. You want to be more involved. Being involved is what convinces you it's actually real, this pregnancy. In this respect (but no other), she has it easier than you. What's theoretical for you is a growing, evolving daily reality for her. She's enjoying (highly debatable) what's called "the mothering privilege": that pregnancy is happening in her body, where she lives, all the time.

She's the one having the cool/awful/interesting/weird/queasy experience. She's the one inventing snacks like pickles wrapped in cheddar cheese. She's the one with the awesome, Marvel-style superhero sense of smell that can catch a whiff of a blocked-up drain three streets away. She's the one the people in white coats keep prodding, poking, monitoring, making charts about.

You might be a bit more panicky and uncertain and future-focused, but otherwise, you're the same you, in the same body, where you live, all the time.

You had hoped pregnancy would bring you and your partner closer, but a lot of the time, it feels more like a wedge pushing you apart.

The Divide, Evelyn and I called it.

There's always been a divide between men and women, of course, but during pregnancy it's perhaps at its widest. Your partner becomes ever more with child while you remain, stubbornly, the same amount of non-pregnant.

You can't close the Divide, but for the good of your relationship, you can narrow it.

There has been a quiet parenting revolution in the past few decades. Supported by new laws equalising maternity and paternity rights and financial aid, and by an understanding of how failing to teach men to be emotionally intelligent, active caregivers has had enormously negative societal effects on everyone, including us men, parents are rethinking outdated, unfair definitions of motherhood and fatherhood.

You intend to be a Modern Father, of course. To offer your child everything your partner will provide—more, even, should your family dynamic call for it. But you can't make a human inside your body.

The Divide irks you.

The best way to narrow it is simply to acknowledge and discuss it, together: how you feel, how she feels, why you rarely feel the same thing, how you're aware that she's doing more of the work, and how keen you are to change that when the baby is out in the world, where you both live, all the time.

A Process, Not an Event

Days pass, don't they? Slowly, those days. They stutter and cough and wheeze by.

Waiting…

Waiting…

Always waiting.

Is it ready yet?

Knock, knock. Can Baby come out and play?

No.

How about now?

Nope.

Soon?

Not a chance.

Her belly slowly swells. As do her breasts. Not that you can get near her breasts. You'd have more luck talking a cumulonimbus cloud down from the sky than talking her into removing her clothes.

You twiddle your thumbs.

You twiddle your balls.

You go to all the appointments with her, of course. Sometimes you're even allowed to sit silently in the corner, like a morose ghost. Sometimes they leave you outside, where you're more like a dog panting its sadness into the waiting room while your lady/master talks to professionals about things beyond your pregnancy pay grade.

No one ever asks about you, do they? Inquires how you're feeling. No, they ask her. All the goddamn time they ask, while prodding, poking, scanning, preening, and fawning all over her. You understand why they ask her, you aren't trying to make everything about you, but still...

"Come on, Dad," she says, when she returns from the doctor's office to find you reading an article about beetroot salads that cure cancer. "Everything's fine. Let's go home."

"Woof," you say. "Woof woof."

You start to doubt, don't you? Will it be any different after the baby is out? Why wouldn't the baby prefer her? Her who has been, for so long, the baby's safe space. Her who is warmer and squishier than you. The one who smells great, even in the morning. The one who's nice to cuddle. The one with the boobs and their life-giving milk.

Parenting is really just another word for *mothering*, you suspect. Men are bozos—just the sperm, the muscle. Tolerated but neither needed nor appreciated.

STOP, DAD!
BAD, DAD!
DOWN, DAD!
DROP THAT DOUBT, DAD.

You couldn't be more wrong. Yes, she's having a different experience right now, but after the birth, everything will change. You will have a specific, important role—a role designed, refined, shaped, polished, and perfected for you.

Don't believe me?

Then you must come with me now on a journey half a

million years into the past to meet our distant ancestor: *Homo heidelbergensis*. H.H. invented fatherhood as we know it.

Before H.H., we had a strict men sire, women rear parenting system. The same you can still find today in most of the animal kingdom. Yes, if you go down to the woods today, you know what won't be a big surprise? Absent fathers. Only 5 percent of male mammals do any active parenting. The reason we do it differently is because of *Homo heidelbergensis*.

There were bipedal hominoids before H.H., but what made H.H. so special was an enormous brain—nearly as big as our own, in fact. Their brains had to be that big because their society, which had both language and fire, was growing ever more complex.

But these huge and still-growing brains were becoming a problem. H.H. was upright now, strutting around on two legs, not bent over on four. In the process, the females' birth canals narrowed.

If the heads of their young grew any larger, it wouldn't be possible to birth them. It was a potentially species-threatening problem. Evolution tried some things and then settled on a brilliant solution: let the brain keep growing after birth. Just throw the baby out early, even if it's completely defenceless and barely even knows it's been born.

The result? Offspring that needed intensive parenting for longer.

Foals can walk within two hours. Humans need a year. And that's just walking—one of dozens of complex skills that we must master. All of which take guidance. H.H.'s mother found that she didn't have time to care for her useless spawn *and* hunt for the protein-rich food she needed for her growing brain. And she couldn't turn to the Sisterhood (more on this later) because they were all busy rearing their own useless progeny. It was a problem nearly as huge as those heads, and fixing it required another drastic change.

What was that change?

We were.

Men.

Evolution took what it had lying around—grunting, fighting, sperm-providing males—and set about moulding us into involved fathers. Another big project. Because in order to motivate us to sacrifice for our young, it would need to ensure we knew which of the clan were ours. Which meant transitioning to monogamous pairs, an arrangement we still (largely) use today. It also altered priorities and personalities by lowering the male's testosterone during the female's pregnancy.

This was radical stuff. Evolution hates big changes. It's parsimonious, as Dr Anna Machin writes in her brilliant book *The Life of Dad*, which covers all this in more detail. "Evolution is obsessively efficient, and it will only lead a species down the route of a complex change in behaviour or anatomy if it is really the only way to ensure the survival of that species. Human fatherhood could be said to be the epitome of such a change... with far-reaching consequences for our species, and it would not have been selected for unless it conferred considerable benefits on us."[1]

Men matter. You have a specific role, and it is hundreds of thousands of years old and vital to our species. As Michin says, "It is a little-known fact, but fathers saved the human race."[2]

I know it may feel as if you're just waiting, nervously stuck in pregnancy limbo, but that's not the case. Because you don't become a father when you first hold your scream-ing, wriggling, afterbirth-splattered baby. Becoming a father is a process, not an event. You have been engaging in it all your life, right from when you were a child watching your father and grandfather and other males parent. Humans are natural mimics. We study and learn from each other. Wanting to ape behaviours you were seeing is probably what resulted in your desire to have a child in the first place, and that desire likely increased during conversations with your partner about what this new adventure might be like. Or perhaps as you watched your siblings and friends start families. Or when you and your partner first tried to conceive (if pregnancy wasn't a happy accident in your case).

The process of becoming a father is accelerating for you now. When your partner became pregnant, her pheromones changed, communicating to your body that she was with child. You might not know it, you might not feel it, but in the cells and pathways of your body and mind enormous hormonal changes are happening, moulding you into the engaged father that *Homo heidelbergensis'* young needed and *Homo sapiens* still depend on today.

You're undergoing the single largest change to your personality since puberty. Evolution is doing its part to close the Divide.

The science of all this is actually pretty remarkable. We've always known that people in close relationships begin to mirror each other's speech, movement, and biological markers, such as heart rate, body temperature, and blood pressure. The term for this is biobehavioural synchrony. What we've only recently discovered is how strong this effect becomes during pregnancy, when there's additional mirroring in oxytocin levels and, as already mentioned, a sharp drop in your testosterone as evolution tries to neuter any wayward instincts, making you less extroverted and more family focused. For a long time, we assumed this was temporary, but we now know your testosterone level will never return to its pre-pregnancy state, regardless of whether you live with your partner and child. Fathers simply have less testosterone than non-fathers.

This isn't bad news. Men whose testosterone levels are lower are more responsive to a child's cry, more willing to coparent, and show more empathy and affection towards their young. The changes happening in your body and mind have already begun and will deepen and intensify as your child grows up. And they're permanent.

Evolution has a specific role for you, similar yet slightly different from the role it has planned for your partner. It will offer neurochemical rewards (mostly oxytocin, serotonin, and dopamine) when you perform specific parenting tasks. You'll get a higher high from rough play than she will. You'll get a higher high from helping your offspring explore and push their physical and social boundaries than she'll receive for being the person they run back to when those explorations go wrong.

Note that in same-sex couples, the two parenting roles (which Michin calls "Safe Harbour" and "Safe Exploration"[3]) are still observably present. The brains of people in same-sex couples just rewire slightly, nudging each parent towards a different role. However, either person can take on either role, always. You're simply more likely to engage in behaviours that offer the highest neurochemical rewards for you.

Many of the hormonal payoffs of fatherhood are already available to you. You can narrow the Divide. When you take time out of your day to think about your unborn child, when you discuss them with your partner, family, or friends, and when you talk to, sing to, or stroke the bump, oxytocin and dopamine will flood your system, helping your attachment deepen.

Take the time. It's worth it. Science shows that fathers who are most attached to their unborn child have the deepest attachment to their child post-birth. Read the bump your favourite book. Every mealtime, make it a ritual to wonder about the person growing in that womb. Will they have your pronounced jaw? Her father's knobbly knees? Your mother's hyena laugh? What adventures will you have together?

You're not waiting. It's already happening. Dad Mode is active. You're a father, even if it doesn't feel like it yet.

Forefathers

It's really easy to forget—because you have four types of yoghurt in your fridge, can fly anywhere in the world at the drop of a hat, and use a bathroom with a heated towel rail—that most of modern human history has been, to use a technical term, a shitshow.

It was in this shitshow that your male ancestors were forced to live and parent. It's no surprise it didn't always go well. As you think about the type of father you want to be, it's important to zoom out a bit and get some perspective on who we are, how we got here, and why we might need to sire the next generation differently. Let's meet our forefathers.

* * *

Great-great-grandfather, Reggie
Born: 1850, Died: 1899

Reggie had a moustache as thick as a rope and a narrow mouth that his pipe never left. He was better with horses than people. He spent his days on the family farm bent like the scythe he often held, trying to encourage potatoes to pop up from the ground. Parenting wasn't a problem for Reggie's generation because few children lived long enough to require any parenting. Childhood was simply the useless period parents endured until their children were old enough to help—to bend over like scythes in the fields and encourage potatoes to pop up from the ground.

Poor old Reg, he was so busy helping his family best another winter, dodge another plague, and hide from another war that there was little time left to help them thrive. That he left to our great-great-grandmother, Philomena, only she was busy beating clothes, cooking stews, cleaning stoves, sewing dresses, and trying not to drown in her daily domestic drudgery. The kids raised themselves and raised each other. You could say it took a village, but they didn't even live in a village.

Many people saw Reggie hit, but not a single person ever saw him cry. Did he love his nine children? Almost certainly. But, also, so what? Love was beyond the point.

What was the point?

Survival.

A pitchfork did old Reggie in. He stood on it one day and the wound in his heel grew infected. Gangrene followed. That was that. He was forty-nine. He'd already been married for twenty-five years. He lived and died within a thirty-mile radius. He fathered as best he knew, but his best wasn't good enough. It wasn't his fault. He was traumatised. Traumatised by death. Traumatised by war. Traumatised by living.

He passed some of it on. He didn't mean to.

* * *

Great-grandfather, Jim
Born: 1888, Died: 1931

Jim was one of three who made it to adulthood. He took over the farm and married a woman from the nearby town. Yes, there were towns now. He and our great-grandmother Tilda had just five children. Jim was his father's son: quick to anger, slow to forgive. He tried to be kinder than his father; he knew a little of emotions but had no time to indulge them —potatoes still weren't growing themselves, even though there were some basic machines to help.

In the quiet moments, between all the plagues and famines and wars, the family would play cards. He'd take Tilda to barn dances and there were even, sometimes, double portions of apple pie. Tilda was still the primary parent, the one the children called out to when they bust open their knees or wet their beds. Jim disciplined when he had to, with his belt or fist, but unlike his father, he always gave a warning first.

He survived the Great War but came home broken, with just one leg and a permanently glazed-over stare. He didn't speak of it but he often shouted about it late into the night. A fire killed him and Tilda as they slept. Only one child was small enough to crawl out through the smoke and collapsed beams.

Jim lived and died within a thousand-mile radius, although he wouldn't have minded if it had been smaller. He did his best, but it was rarely good enough. It wasn't his fault. He was traumatised. Traumatised by death. Traumatised by war. Traumatised by living.

He passed some of it on. He didn't mean to.

* * *

Grandfather, John
Born: 1920, Died: 1995

John grew up in a boys' home under the strictest of discipline. He had a scar that resembled lightning across his chest from the fire that killed his family. He was bullied mercilessly both at home and at school. Cities were sprouting up like weeds and he hid in one as soon as he could. There, he made screws on a factory lathe ten hours a day, six days a week. He was going steady with Sarah, the woman who would become our grandmother, when he got the letter that said his country needed him to kill strangers in foreign lands. Another war, you see. An even greater one. Don't worry, they reassured him, you're one of the good guys. Now get out there, soldier, go do some murdering.

Somehow, although almost everyone else died, John survived. He often wished he hadn't. He came home traumatised and found everyone else traumatised. They didn't talk about the war. They didn't talk about anything that mattered. It was too painful, and they didn't know how much it helped, yet. John hid in a bottle and never came out. The children were too much for him. He had no patience, was quicker to anger than both his father and his grandfather. Sarah was the caregiver. When John was home, he struggled to show kindness and love. He never used the L-word, either. He lived long enough for cancer to kill him at age seventy-five, which was progress, of sorts. He lived and died within a five-thousand-mile radius, although he would have loved it to have been smaller. He did his best, but it was rarely good enough. It wasn't his fault. He was heavily traumatised. Traumatised by death. Traumatised by war. Traumatised by living.

He passed some of it on. He didn't mean to.

* * *

Father, Peter
Born: 1955, Died:

Born into a wrecked world that had to be rebuilt, Peter was the first child to know excess—to grow up in boom times. Everything was becoming mechanised. Workers' blue collars were turning white. He took an internship at an engineering firm. Yes, an office, a sterile place with padded chairs, health and safety monitors, and eye-wash stations. Science led his generation, and the social sciences followed closely behind. When he had children, he vowed to be better than the men of his bloodline. He knew that emotions mattered. That he should cuddle and treasure his young. He earned so much money that his wife, Veronica, didn't have to work at all in her children's formative years. Instead, she ironed his shirts, cooked his dinners, and carried the family's mental load, which, while heavy, was lighter than that of the women in her bloodline. She was the person her children called out to first, but Peter was there too, a fine substitute. Peter mopped brows, changed bed sheets, and cooked fish fingers and French fries. He even told us he loved us, occasionally, at major life events. He rarely hit his children, and if he did, it was a quick spank after many warnings, and meant to shock, not injure.

With so few children, he and Veronica invested in them greatly and never wanted to let them go.

Peter has lived within a thousand-mile radius, and he might yet make it bigger. He's thinking about a safari in South Africa. He did his best. It was good enough.

* * *

You and me

We've joined this big human experiment at a very interesting time. Modernity is moving at warp speed. Women are demanding the rights we have long held. The game has changed—and apparently, we're no longer allowed to flagrantly cheat at it. We're awake, and sometimes even woke. Men of the world, we cook Chinese food, dress in French shirts, and dance to Latin music while chugging Scottish whisky. We (hopefully) no longer hit, haze, and harass. We live in the light. We love freely. We want to be judged by our brain as much as our brawn. We have seen the commendable work our father, Peter, did and want to build upon it.

We know that the job we're applying for, Modern Father, is new and poorly defined. We know that it challenges the orthodoxy of the last half-dozen generations (more on how this role differs from that of a 1950s Father shortly). We want our children to know emotional excess, to feel that our love for them is unconditional, that it burns within us with the intensity of a thousand suns. They will learn, through our example, that there is no shame in feeling nor in expressing emotions. That it's our vulnerability that makes us human, not our strength. And that without each other, we are nothing.

* * *

Our sons and daughters

They will be lucky to have us. We will be luckier still to have them. We can't wait to meet them. It's going to be so, so great.

Job Vacancy:
1950s Father - PART TIME

Status Quo has a vacancy for a 1950s Father, a part-time position in a soon-to-be established traditional family unit. This rewarding role requires an uncompromising alpha male to lead a God-fearing, monogamous (wink, wink, boys will be boys, wink wink), heterosexual home in which your word is law. Under your unswerving guidance, the home's 2.1 children, hired domestic help, and unpaid female serf (official title: Wife) will achieve excellence as you define it.
While quitting is frowned upon, there is the possibility to abscond to somewhere warmer with your secretary.

Hours:
10 to 15 (at weekends, but tasks can be completed when hungover and sullen).

Location:
An attractive, cookie-cutter suburb. Your picket fence will be the whitest in the neighbourhood. An automobile will provide convenient access to your job in the city and to essential services such as supermarkets, pubs, and mistresses.

Responsibilities:
- Strict supervision of Wife, who must perform domestic, culinary, clerical, and sexual duties to your satisfaction, *dammit*.
- Regular contribution of sperm to Wife, aiding creation of at least 2.1 children (males preferred).
- Financial provision and administration of home and dependents; distribution of both pocket and buy-yourself-something-pretty money.

- Education/indoctrination of all household members regarding societal gender norms.
- Household discipline (corporal punishment both allowed and encouraged).
- Strict emotional absenteeism (to avoid the curse of the mollycoddle).

About you:
You enjoy smoking cigars, doffing hats, espousing opinions, and drinking liquor. You aren't afraid to put women and children in their place (seen but not heard). Your word is final, always. You have a belt and you're not afraid to use it. You were born and will die in a buttoned-up shirt. You possess only three emotions: horny, hungry, and hotheaded. You are a graduate of the Go Ask Your Mother school of delegation. You moustache with commendable enthusiasm.

Modern Father - Full Time

Post-Patriarchy Plc has a vacancy for the position of Modern Father in a soon-to-be established non-traditional family unit. This is a challenging, stereotype-defying role to be defined in collaboration with the other half of the family leadership-and-coparenting team.

You will be required to communicate non-violently at all times, smash the patriarchy, parent gently, cry even when onions aren't near, regularly admit you were wrong, nurture but let thrive, be permissive but consistent, and give without demand.

The position is full-time, unpaid, and cannot be quit, ever.

Hours:
40 to 120 (you are expected to do 50 percent of all household drudgery and parenting, perhaps more, if circumstances require it).

Location:
A modern, urban city/hellscape. You'll enjoy the use of a gardenless, boxy apartment. A bicycle will be provided for you to reach essential services such as playgrounds, soft-play centres, trees, and therapists.

Responsibilities:
- Offer love, respect, emotional nourishment, and back rubs to all household members, including partner(s), child(ren), pets, and plants.
- Create/adopt/foster/uncle/godfather/coparent/social-

parent one or more children; this will involve extensive down-on-the-carpet play, finger-painting, cuddling, tuck-ins, Duplo dazzlement, and pretend pony school.
- Contribute at least 50 percent to total finance, maintenance, childcare, emotional-load, and packed-lunch needs.
- Be willing to have fingernails and toenails painted.

About you:
You are a graduate of the School of Life. You pray nightly to Esther Perel. You own at least two Ottolenghi cookbooks. You're fluent in the canons of Disney, Pixar, and Mattel. You embrace your contradictions, trying to be strong and soft, firm and fair, decisive and inclusive, and patient and not a pushover. You don't believe any word is final except, perhaps, "I love you."

The Sacred Sisterhood

By the end of the first trimester, Evelyn and I had settled into our new roles. Hers was lying on the sofa complaining about all her various bodily discomforts and the world's aggressive smells, laughing in the face of my physical overtures, and shouting for all the things she wanted delivered to her, by me, RIGHT NOW.

I'd started a few fatherhood books, abandoned them, and then returned to my normal life as a hermit workaholic constantly interrupted by his girlfriend shouting for all the things she wanted delivered to her, by him, RIGHT NOW.

One day, having seen a For Sale post on a neighbourhood app, I went to find Evelyn.

"Baby bath?" I said, angling my head around the living room door. "A neighbour's selling one for five euros, but that seems excessive, since we already have a bath?"

"Hang on," she said, tapping on her phone before putting it back on her lap into a nest of biscuit wrappers. "Do I hear the ding of the microwave?"

"You do not."

Her head tilted. "Why not, though?"

29

"Because I haven't put the lasagne in it yet, that's why not."

"Why not, though?"

"Stop saying 'Why not, though'."

"Well, stop not heating the lasagne then."

Her phone trilled. She picked it up and looked at the screen. "No," she said, putting it back down. "Don't need."

"Lasagne?"

"Baby bath."

"Okay. Cool." I lingered in the doorway.

"Anything else?" she asked. "Because *Emily in Paris* isn't going to watch itself."

"There's no way you just asked the Internet about baby baths," I said. "Because I ask the Internet stuff all the time but answers come at the end of four-hour long binges and are enormously hyperbolic. I leave less informed than I go in."

She smiled. "There's this group thing."

I lurched into the room. "It's a cult, isn't it? How much have you given them?"

"No," she said. "A WhatsApp group."

"A cult WhatsApp group?"

"A pregnant women WhatsApp group. Sara added me."

"Hmm," I said, my eyes narrowing. Sara was her sister and a very reasonable person, certainly not someone prone to cults, unless you consider Tupperware a cult, and I suppose the jury is still out.

"Fine," I said, and went to the kitchen to stoically fulfil the latest of her many whims.

Over the next weeks, I noticed her consulting with this group more and more often. The Sacred Sisterhood, we started calling it. Its answers always came near-instantly but seemed both extensively researched and even-handedly presented. By the end of her pregnancy, she'd even become an administrator of her own chapter of it, here in Berlin: a dozen pregnant women, less pregnant than Evelyn, all full of the same questions she'd had, trading information, resources, hopes, fears, and maternity wear.

It was beautiful to watch.

I was in a tight Brotherhood too, of course, having nodded six times at the man with the toddler in the other part of our apartment complex. By the time our kids were in school, we'd definitely have exchanged names.

First names.

"It seems like men would rather fail alone than succeed together," Evelyn said one day.

"That sounds about right."

"Why?"

"I don't know," I said. "Testosterone? Toxic masculinity? Being raised not to show vulnerability and emotion?"

"It sucks."

"It's changing," I said. "But not fast enough."

You can help with that change. It's still the first trimester. You have time and energy and can invest in friendships. You can begin a chapter of the Brotherhood. Even if you feel as though you don't need help now, because your life is still mostly as it was, after the birth, that life will be gone forever. What's coming is going to be really, really hard. And even when it's not, it will often be quite boring. There's only so much novelty you can rinse from pushing a tiny person on a swing eight thousand times in a row. I don't know if a problem shared is really a problem halved, but boredom shared is very often no longer boredom at all.

Don't make the same mistake I did. Invest in friendships with other expecting parents now—especially dads—before you need them.

We need to be more like our women.

31

SuperSmeller

"I'm seriously considering walking around with a peg on my nose," Evelyn said, as we hurried to the brunch we were so late for it had almost become a lunner.

"We'd be there by now if you'd let us take the subway," I said.

"People stink, do you know that? I had no idea. *Ugh*."

"I don't stink."

She sniffed. "You are a bit pongy, actually."

I put my nose inside my jumper. "You used to love my smell."

She shrugged. "I think I will again. But right now, it's like the whole world is rotting."

We turned a corner and arrived on a street full of halal butchers, shisha lounges, and falafel restaurants. She grabbed my arm. "Not this way."

"Why?"

She pointed. "Bins. Let's go back."

"But the other way's even longer."

"Would you rather be late because of a detour or because I puked down a drain?"

"Fine," I said. "How long does SuperSmell last? It's getting kind of old."

"Old for you? What about me?"

I shrugged. "Mothering privilege, isn't it?"

She rolled her eyes. "Some women have it all the way through. For others, it lasts just a month or two."

"I'm sorry," I said, taking her hand, which she pulled away so she could pinch her nose as we passed two split plastic bags of rubbish leaking ooze into the road.

"Me too," she said.

It's likely that your partner will have periods of Super-Smell, particularly in the first trimester. Hyperosmia, it's called. Studies vary, but in one study 67 percent of women reported some increase in olfactory sensitivity.[1] Perhaps because of hormonal changes, or perhaps, with the pregnancy still somewhat fragile and the consequences of ingesting harmful bacteria high, a female's body protects itself by cranking up her sense of smell.

A rubbish truck pulled onto the pavement in front of us. "Oh god," she said, running in the other direction.

I chased after her and tried to slow her down. "I have to go home," she said. "It's just too strong today."

"What about brunch?" I asked.

"I've lost my appetite."

"Okay," I said. "We're really late now anyway. I'll text them and blame the pregnancy."

"We're playing that card a lot."

"It's a good card. Having young kids will be an even better one."

"Kid," she said.

"Right. *Yep.*"

"What if everyone stops inviting us places?"

"They'll all have kids soon too," I said. "They'll need us. We'll need each other."

"I'm going to try the peg."

"Try the peg." I pointed to a nearby restaurant. "I'll just nip in and get a kebab."

"Ugh," she said again. It was becoming her pregnancy catchphrase. "Will you eat it on the other side of the road?"

"It's a kebab, not a poop sandwich."

"Fine," she said. "But no onions."

Part Two
The Second Trimester
The Public Pregnancy

Am I a Bad Parent?

It's evening, and the subway train rattles as it decelerates into the next station, just three away from your house. The doors whoosh open and a sad, hunched husk of a man shoves in a pram the size of a jumbo jet. Inside of it, a baby screams louder than one.

Reflexively, you cover your ears as you notice all the various distraction devices hanging off this death-star on wheels: birds on rods, an elephant on a bungee cord, and some bright textile squares covered in mirrors. You think about how dog toys and infant toys are indistinguishable then remember a YouTube video about pigs and toddlers that taught you how smart bacon used to be.

It's why you no longer eat it.

The man does nothing, tries nothing, offers nothing to appease his wailing infant.

Bad parent, you think.

You meet the man's eyes, noting that the bags beneath them are large enough to hold your weekly shopping. He yawns, this part-man, part-wither, not even bothering to cover his mouth.

Bad human, you think.

He stares through you. If the lights in his eyes are on, they're certainly too dim to read by.

Rather you than me, buddy, you say to yourself, relaxing deeper into your chair, excited for an evening of making dinner, making conversation, making music, ~~making love~~ masturbating. You have no fixed plans, are happy to be buffeted by the winds of whim, and then… BOOM. You remember. *It's going to be me.*

You're going to become this man. She's pregnant. You're going to be a dad. In many ways, physically and emotionally, you already are one.

You forgot again, didn't you?

How does that keep happening, even so late into the first trimester? The all-important twelve-week scan is just next week. And yet, you think about your day—that big shiny expanse of time you so exquisitely squandered fretting about the wording of a client e-mail, back hair, and a person called Glenn who wronged you in high school, a slight still unavenged—and you realise that not even once did you think about your baby-to-be, busy kicking your girlfriend in the guts, like some kind of tiny hooligan drunk on amniotic fluid.

And then a thought crashes in: *Am I already a bad parent?*

Welcome to the club, chief.

That notion, well, get used to it. You've experienced it a touch earlier than most, perhaps, but once the littlun is out here, in the world, it's going to be omnipresent in your mind. Because no matter how much you're bubble-bathing, finger-painting, crayoning, bum-wiping, nursery-rhyme singing, and hide-and-seeking, you'll know—just like this man in front of you with the crying baby knows—there is more you *could* give were you not too exhausted, bored, unmotivated, resentful, or sad.

For much of the early parenting years, you will be physically there but mentally far away, the lights in your eyes dim too, as you're pitied by strangers, just like…

You lift your hands from your ears. Your face softens into a smile. You get up, walk over, clasp him on the shoulder, and say: "You've lost today, buddy, but tomorrow is a new day. Tomorrow is yours. Just you wait and see."

He's not a bad parent. He's just a parent.

The Magic Milestone

One of the best things about pregnancy is that you get to tell people you're/she's/we're pregnant (depending on your pronoun of choice—more on this shortly)

They bloody love getting the news, they do. They get so excited. There's hugging. Tears. You're bathed in loving attention. Celebratory drinks and food are ordered. They usually pick up the tab.

But before you enjoy all that, you must decide *when* you're going to tell people the good news.

It's a more fraught decision than you might think.

When I was growing up (in the UK), my family moved our birthdays around. No one wanted a Wednesday birthday, so we'd either shove the happy day forwards or backwards to a weekend, depending on the needs of our calendars and the flippancy of the weather forecast.

Other families seemed to do this too. It was normal. As much as anything is normal. Then I moved to Germany, where I promptly discovered one does not just casually rearrange the celebration of one's earthly arrival. You tumbled out of your mother on a specific date. That date is fact. There were witnesses. Forms. Certificates. Afterbirth.

Worse than that, Germans think the act of wishing you well a few days early is such terrible luck, you will almost certainly die before the correct date arrives. Accordingly, no one here moves their birthday, regardless how Wednesday it is. Or not forwards, anyway. Culture and tradition are powerful, even if they don't always make rational sense.

Bear this in mind when deciding when to tell people. Tradition, that stickler, says you should wait until after the twelve-week scan. But the times, as a man called Bob once sang, they are a-changin'.

Why?

Pregnancy tests are becoming more and more sensitive, which means they can detect pregnancies earlier, meaning many women discover they are briefly "chemically pregnant" before losing that pregnancy (often because of a shortage of progesterone or because the embryo wasn't viable). In the past, they might not have noticed this happening.

Now they notice, and it hurts.

Evelyn had several of these chemical pregnancies, and one later miscarriage during the first trimester (reliable data on miscarriage rates is hard to find, in the UK, The National Childbirth Trust reports the odds of miscarriage as 25 percent at four weeks; 5 percent at eight weeks; 1.7 percent at 12 weeks, so those even earlier miscarriages we had were not uncommon at all[1]). Each time, however brief the pregnancy, the loss gutted us. We didn't mourn the loss of the handful of cells, but we mourned the loss of what they could have become. Meanwhile, our fears grew. We feared it was never going to work out. We feared that something in one of us, or in the combination of us, was broken beyond repair.

And even worse, we had to mourn and feel that fear all alone.

None of our close friends or family could console us, as none of them knew Evelyn had been (briefly) pregnant—because tradition said that it was too soon to tell them and that miscarriage, however early, is a private matter.

There's a movement encouraging women (and men) to more openly discuss difficulties regarding conceiving and failed pregnancies.

This is, undoubtedly, a good thing.

During Evelyn's last pregnancy—which was the result of IVF, so we knew there was a top-notch egg in there—we decided not to wait. In fact, within twenty-four hours of the positive test,[2] we'd already told 75 percent of all the humans we'd ever met, including those we'd shared an elevator with, once, in 1994.

Okay, I'm exaggerating. Maybe it was 50 percent. It would have been more, had we not received some adverse reactions to our supposedly good news. When I told my friend Toby, he stuttered like a malfunctioning robot. Eventually, he recovered enough to tell me how annoyed he was that I'd told him because it was obviously too early and now he didn't know how he was supposed to react.

There were several awkward exchanges like this. People seemed to feel that by breaking the twelve-week rule, like breaking the birthday rule in Germany, we were embroiling them in some kind of jinxing conspiracy. So we stopped telling people and waited for the twelve-week Magic Milestone, like everyone else.

It's Not What You Feel

You're in the doctor's office—it's finally time for that twelve-week scan. If this goes well, you'll have crossed the Magic Milestone. You're already imagining all the fun ways you're going to break the news to people. The doctor covers your partner's belly with that weird jelly stuff, rubs her with the alien dildo wand, and you have the crystal-clear realisation you're in a key life moment. A staple of popular culture, so regularly depicted in movies. A rite of passage. You lean in. This is something you're never going to forget.

Pushing the wand around, the doctor stares at the screen. There's a sound. A fast-paced beating.

Thud-thud-thud-thud-thud-thud.

It's almost technolike, that beating. The doctor turns the monitor towards you both. You stare at the grainy blob floating and flickering like a ghost in a washing machine.

Thud-thud-thud-thud-thud-thud.

"Lovely heartbeat," the doctor says, and your partner squeezes your hand. You smile reflexively, yet to your shock and horror, you feel... almost nothing?

Oh no.

Is this not further evidence of your empathic absence?

Your rotten core?

Your deep inner deadness?

You keep smiling, keep squeezing her hand, because what else can you do? Yawn? Nip out for a sandwich?

Thud-thud-thud-thud-thud-thud.

The doctor is humming quietly as he clicks and draws lines, measuring the distances between things, measuring the size of the head and the width of the neck of what everyone but you is convinced is your future child.

Thud-thud-thud-thud-thud-thud.

You wish you had their conviction. This was supposed to be an amazing moment, and yet, scanning yourself, you still feel... almost nothing.

Eventually, a feeling arrives: sadness laced with disappointment and wrapped in fear. Because what if you're still like this after the birth? What if you never bond with your baby?

You will. And you're not broken, champ.

Well, no more broken than many of us. Until that baby is in our hands, screaming into our faces, it's hard for a lot of us men to truly accept that it exists. But I assure you it really is in there and it does already have fingernails and hair and can suck its thumb and in just two trimesters it really will be out here. Then all of this, everything that came before—good, bad, indifferent, climactic, anti-climactic, genuine, forced—will slip into the shadows of time.

Until then, go through the motions, acting as you want to feel. For some of us, that helps. It's like worshippers in a mega-church trying to speak in tongues. For some, the pressure to do it is what makes it happen, what hits their accelerators. For the rest of us, that pressure slams on our brakes. If that's you, take the pressure off yourself—it's not what you feel that matters but what you feel about what you feel (or in this case, what you don't feel quite yet). Just keep turning up every day and at every major marker, every pop-culture milestone, every rite of passage, ready to feel. Ready to feel whatever you're feeling.

"That really is an exquisite heartbeat," the doctor says, grinning at you. "Good job."

"Thanks," you say.

Thud-thud-thud-thud-thud-thud.

We're Pregnant

You've crossed the Magic Milestone and are now free to tell people, if you haven't already. Now, in this hypermodern time of hyperpronoun individualism, you must decide if you're going to go with *"we're* pregnant" or *"she's* pregnant."

In my experience, about 50 percent of couples adopt *we*, while the other half laugh mercilessly at them.

As revealed by the conversation in our kitchen, back when I tried to give up alcohol, Evelyn was very much in the latter group. For her, my saying "we're pregnant" was like footballer John Terry, suspended from the 2012 Champions League final, stripping down to his kit, spraying himself with water to make it look as if he were sweating, and then jumping into the celebration photos when his team won.

We weren't pregnant. *She* was pregnant

But then, as is her nature, Evelyn read every single pregnancy book published in the past twenty years. Twice. She likes research; it calms her down. While reading, she'd pepper me with the best anecdotes. This was how I learned about couvade syndrome, a French term that roughly translates to, yep, *we're pregnant.*

Apparently, up to 59 percent of men experience some kind of pregnancy-symptom sharing[1]. If their partner's stomach cramps, their stomach cramps. Their better half vomits before breakfast, they do too. The way Evelyn described it, it sounded kind of nice. I pictured her and me, side by side in front of the porcelain throne, bent forwards like question marks, taking turns holding each other's hair as we expelled our breakfasts in violent gusts.

Not that I have any hair. I'd put on a wig.

Anyway, after reading more about the syndrome and hearing the stories of its sufferers, we both came to realise something important: *we're pregnant* is not a statement of biological fact but a statement of desire. An honest attempt to narrow the Divide. Many men want to catch couvade, want to be more involved—even if that means dry heaving every time they smell eggs.

And that's kind of beautiful, no?

"You can use *we*, if you want," Evelyn said one day, early into the second trimester.

"Thanks," I said. "But it's okay. *You're* pregnant. *We're* expecting."

We're Pregnant too

In the animal kingdom some defenceless animals such as gazelles give birth together, flooding the savannah with their young. While most will be eaten, there will be such a glut of baby gazelles that a few will survive past infancy and grow to become adults. At this point, if they're female, their reproductive cycles will sync and… repeat.

Whenever you decide to tell people, you can expect at least one couple in your social circle to giggle nervously and then, gazelle-like, reveal that they too are pregnant. They just hadn't wanted to say anything because they hadn't passed the Magic Milestone yet.

Every couple in a friend group who becomes pregnant doubles the likelihood of another pair deciding that this is the moment to start their family. There's a sense that the road is about to fork. We want to stay with the people we care about. The idea, having children, that used to seem so ridiculous, fanciful, and distant, can't be—as the people we love, respect, and fill our weekends with are all doing it.

The more the merrier. Having a child is socially isolating, especially if, like Evelyn and me, you're one of those stupid, idealistic, young experience seekers who fled far away from your family to live in Really Far Away Big Ugly Metropolis—the rent, the rent, the rent is too high—and now have too much career, too many friends, and too little sanity to leave. As a result, you have no family within six hours to come help you raise the next generation.

Other than your friends. Whom you won't see much unless they also have children. Your daily rhythm is about to change enormously, from one built around the nine-to-five workday to one built around the energy and sleep cycles of a tiny, erratic human who lives entirely in the present.

Cool, childless people don't want to come to the playground at 7am to play in the sandpit. Cool, childless people don't eat crustless-ham-sandwich lunches at 10:45am. Cool, childless people aren't waiting outside the kids' museum at 9am, in the rain, only to rush home to eat crustless sandwiches again at 11:30 before The Nap—the best two hours of the entire day. Nor are they falling asleep on the couch at 8:30pm, ninety minutes into a *Peppa Pig* marathon.

Gazelles are. And you're going to need each other.

What Happens When Again?

You've crossed the Magic Milestone and told everyone. It'll be smooth sailing from here, right? Erm... well... no, probably not. Let's take a closer look at what's coming.

Second trimester: sunshine with a chance of mania

Mother: Studies show that most parents-to-be like the second trimester best. Things are settling down for her hormonally, as her body has learned to do its new job. From week sixteen, the placenta will be fully formed and providing nutrients and oxygen to the growing foetus. So, if you're lucky, all the early queasiness will have passed. Her belly will grow—and if you're both lucky, so will her energy levels. It's also the trimester where couples report having the most normal sex life. Enjoy that before the baby destroys it.

In this trimester, she'll become visibly pregnant, which is great. She'll get many positive reactions. Everyone will want to know how it's going and how long's left. Cars will drive slower. Seats will be given up on the subway. People will smile more. She'll get the prestige but without the slog of carrying a near-term baby.

That said, towards the end of the second trimester, the child might already be big enough to trigger the first leg cramps, backaches, swollen feet, and round-ligament pain: a sharp ache in a lower abdomen, which has stretched to support the uterus. Good thing you're an excellent masseuse, right?

No, really, learn how to massage. It'll be really helpful in the third trimester and during the birth.

Baby: Vast changes are happening this trimester, including, between weeks thirteen and sixteen, the growth of hair and teeth. Baby is going to move around more, which Mum is going to find so, so fun. Not. Increasingly, hanging out with them will be like watching two angry motorists fighting over a parking space. One of those motorists is about to learn how to swallow, so that's nice. Oh, and by about week fifteen, it will be able to hear you, too. Speak up and speak often. This really helps the bond.

Around weeks seventeen to twenty, it's going to get grabby. And if you've talked at or around it enough, it will recognise the soft, sultry baritone of your voice.

In weeks twenty-one to twenty-four, its brain will develop rapidly. It will move its eyes, blink and taste, and will be about the size of a grapefruit. You'll be two-thirds of the way there. *Hurrah.*

The Pregnancy Spectrum

In our friend circle, three women fell pregnant at the same time. They were all German, middle class, and of a similar age, upbringing, schooling, and temperament.

The first to get pregnant, Linda, had a horrendous time. She was bedridden from about week three. If she lifted her head, she vomited. If she ate, she vomited. When she didn't eat, she... didn't vomit, but also didn't get to eat. Then she got pneumonia, but the doctor decided she couldn't have medication for it—not because there was any definitive proof medication could cause a problem with the pregnancy, but because it was "better to be on the safe side" (more on this later).

Only it wasn't better. Her pneumonia got worse until she was hospitalised and a doctor, looking at the state of her lungs, told her she was lucky to be alive and then gave her the medication the previous doctor had denied her.

She got better, thankfully, and the baby came out just fine.

Evelyn had a fairly average pregnancy, loathing it but

finding it mostly manageable, as long as I stayed far away from her. It was complicated by a hematoma, which meant she was signed off work early and had to rest much more than she would have liked to. She endured pregnancy, but she wouldn't recommend it to anyone and never wants to do it again. When she talks about it now, she cringes, as if it were a terrible boyfriend she's embarrassed to have dated.

The third of our friends, Petra, had, and I quote, "the greatest time." As did anyone near her. It was as if she radiated oxytocin. She was completely in love with the universe and her partner and the child growing inside her.

Why am I telling you these three very different stories?

Precisely because of their differences. Even if things get calmer for your partner in the second trimester, know that there's an enormously wide spectrum of experience in pregnancy, just as in every area of life. Still, people—and since you've told everyone now, there's all this advice, all these opinions and friends-of-friends anecdotes incoming—are going to try to suggest that your partner is responsible for the type of pregnancy she's having.

She's not.

Linda didn't have a terrible pregnancy because she did something wrong—i.e. didn't eat well enough, exercised too much, or wasn't in a positive mental state (she went on to have a second child, and with it, pretty much exactly the same pregnancy minus the pneumonia). Nor was Petra's dream pregnancy the result of something she did correctly. Your partner has no control over where they'll fall on the pregnancy spectrum, just as you have no control over the population of Singapore, how much she'll need you during the pregnancy, or what that need (or lack of) makes you feel. Evelyn and I both would have preferred a pregnancy where we could have touched occasionally, but alas, it wasn't meant to be. Guilting her about what she couldn't change wouldn't have helped anyone.

It's all just a crapshoot.

All you can do is try to support her as best you can, with whatever her biology throws at her.

Halloumi

It's Saturday and you're in the kitchen, at the stove, frying up halloumi for a salad. She couldn't sleep last night, said she felt like a boat on stormy seas. Cooking her a light, healthy lunch is really the least you can do. As the halloumi hisses and crackles in the pan, you feel good about yourself and the future.

There's a knock on the door.

You sigh. There have been a lot of knocks on the door since you told everyone she's pregnant. You open it. An impossibly old woman stands there—a hundred if she's a day —in a tightly buttoned-up cardigan, nostrils flaring.

"IF YOU SERVE HER HALLOUMI, YOUR BABY WILL DIE," she says.

You take a half-step back. "Who are you?"

"Jim's wife."

"Who's Jim?"

"DO YOU WANT YOUR BABY TO DIE?"

You wipe a little olive oil from your hands onto the tea towel hanging over your shoulder. "Stop shouting. And our baby is not going to die."

"Sheila from the village over the hill ate one piece of halloumi when she was pregnant and her baby came out with two heads."

"Wait. I thought it makes babies die?"

She flicks her hand dismissively. "It died later, okay? First, it had two heads. Do you want your baby to have two heads?" She sniffs. "And is that egg I smell? Pregnant women can't eat eggs."

"They can. I checked the science."

"SCIENCE SCHMIENCE."

"The salmonella risk is like one serving in a thousand," you say, in protest. "It's a rounding error. She can eat eggs."

"You're a rounding error," she says. "No eggs. No salmon. No raw fish. All these rules exist for a reason. It's ancient wisdom."

"They exist because even people who mean well can do harm," you say. "And because stories are more compelling than stats." You take a deep breath. "Look, Jim's

Wife, I can see that you care. That you're coming from a good place. Jim's lucky to have you, but my partner loves halloumi and so, pregnant or not, she's going to eat halloumi, okay?"

"BABY KILLER," she hisses.

You slam the door in her face.

"Another old wife?" your partner asks. "What was her tale?"

"Halloumi."

"But I love halloumi."

"You're getting halloumi," you say, and return to the stove.

Global Baby Defenders

It was the middle of the second trimester. In our living room, we were having a get-to-know-you session with our new midwife, whom Evelyn had met via... try to guess. Yep. The Sacred Sisterhood.

I'd expected an esoteric, frumpy middle-aged woman who crocheted children's berets and sold them on Etsy, but the person on the other side of the table was younger than we were, hipper than we were, heavily tattooed, and absurdly knowledgeable.

Midwives are well trained, so finding the right one, which you should do about now, is mostly about alignment. In other words, do you have the same values and beliefs? Our midwife, Marina, talked a lot about "the scientific consensus" and "all available research suggesting" and not about tradition or expectation or anything New of Age. There's nothing wrong with these things, of course—Evelyn and I just aren't wired this way. Which was why we recognised how lucky we'd been to find a midwife with similar circuitry. And when I say *we*, I mean, of course, that Evelyn found her.

"If you have questions from now on," Marina said, "ask

me first. I know you normally ask the Internet things, but"—
she licked her lips—"parent Internet is not like the normal
Internet. Have you noticed that?"

"We've noticed that," Evelyn said, and we all laughed.

Probably you've noticed it too, but if not, let me explain.
During the pregnancy, it's likely you'll end up in a situation
that makes you wonder. Say you're at a birthday party and
there's a bouncy castle and you both feel like a jump and
wrestle but wonder, *Is that dangerous? Could it cause a
miscarriage?*

You don't think so, but you've heard so many old wives'
tales, so many horror stories about friends of friends, you no
longer trust your instincts. So, your partner casually pulls
out her phone and googles it. She ends up on social media or
some random mummy forum. Her eyes bulge. Her mouth
narrows. "These bitches are crazy," she says, slipping the
phone back into her handbag, having experienced Pregnancy
& Parenting Internet (PPI), a hissing, heckling snake pit of
hysteria. The place Marina was warning us about.

A place you both need to be careful of. In person, people
are cautious with their opinions, but online, hidden behind a
veil of anonymity, they let out all their rage, judgement, and
irrationality.

Unborn babies and children can't protect themselves, so
it's understandable that everyone becomes protective of
them. Some people, however, become too protective. They
become self-appointed members of the Global Baby Defenders, a private, well-armed motherhood militia that roams the
Internet.

Global Baby Defenders are women, almost always. Often,
they are mothers. A particular type of mother, I imagine.
One whose children breastfed until they were five, coslept
until they were twelve, and were homeschooled until they
were twenty-five.

They love their children. They love their children too much. They're triggered easily. Don't seem to understand why people might want a life, career, hobbies, interests outside of motherhood. They certainly never dared to do that. Is no one thinking of the poor, defenceless children?

They're thinking of them. It's all they're thinking about. Not their own children—they're in college or therapy or whatever. No, it's other people's defenceless, innocent spawn who keep them tapping at their keyboards in the early-morning glow, answering questions from nervous pregnant women wanting to know if it's okay to eat raw salad or wrestle on a bouncy castle.

What do they say, these Global Baby Defenders?

They say no.

Or, more precisely, they shout NO and then, in an all-caps screed, character-assassinate the callous, selfish woman who has dared to ask this.

And why wouldn't they say no? What does it cost them, this no?

It costs them nothing. So, why take a risk when a child, born or unborn, is involved? They certainly didn't take any risks. They are not for the taking of risks.

In 2002, British comedian Dave Gorman popularised the search-engine sport of Googlewhacking: finding two-word combinations that resulted in a solitary Google result. It's hard to estimate how many hours of office productivity were lost to the game, but it played a significant role in my need to repeat an entire year of college.

It was after we discovered just how wild PPI is—and, I suppose, once we didn't need it any more because we had Marina and the Sisterhood—that we adapted Mr Gorman's game, calling it Miscarriagewhack. Whenever we were bored, we'd think of the most ridiculous thing that surely nobody on earth could believe might cause a miscarriage, then we'd Google it. If we couldn't find a Global Baby Defender in a forum shouting at a pregnant woman considering doing it, we'd win.

We almost never won. Global Baby Defenders are everywhere, and they are prolific.

Oh, but the rabbit holes we went down. *Napkin + Miscarriage* led Evelyn into a motherhood forum where a newly pregnant woman knew, rightly, that she wasn't supposed to eat raw meat. Then she went to a Greek restaurant with her husband. He ate a Gyros plate (i.e. most cooked meat ever). She then accidentally used *his* napkin to wipe *her* mouth and lost two nights of sleep from fear that she'd harmed her unborn child. She wanted reassurance that this wasn't the case, but she didn't understand where she was, whom she was talking to.

The response she got from the caring people of PPI? Five words: "JUST DON'T DO IT AGAIN."

Default Do

The problem of over caution isn't restricted to at-home amateurs. During the second trimester, Evelyn was having terrible migraines and went to a doctor, who was nice and sympathetic and had excellent hair with a natural kink. I don't know why she insists on telling me about other men's hair. I've wandered off topic.

"Obviously, I'd usually refer you for an MRI scan," this doctor said. "But what with you being, you know." He made a half circle over his stomach.

"Oh," Evelyn said. "Pregnant women can't have MRI scans?"

"They can," he said. "It's perfectly safe."

Her eyes narrowed. "So…?"

"You probably want to wait, though, right? Just to be on the safe side?"

"But I'm having the migraines now."

"You could have the scan, of course. I just assumed what with you being…" He trailed off.

"Pregnant?" she asked, wondering why this word was being avoided. "But you said it's safe?"

"Yes, yes," he said, wafting his hand. "Perfectly safe."

"Okay. Then can I have the scan?"

His voice firmed. "You're sure you want the scan?"

"Is there a reason I should be unsure?"

"No."

"Well, I'm sure, I guess?"

He gave her a referral. Two weeks later, she walked into a specialist clinic, which looked largely the same as the other clinic but had more attractive plants. The receptionist tapped at her computer and pulled up Evelyn's file. Evelyn turned to the side to admire the thick foliage on one of those plants.

"You're *pregnant*," the receptionist said, as if the word were on fire. "Are you sure you want an MRI?"

"My doctor said it was safe."

The receptionist nodded. "Totally safe. It's just, well, you could wait?"

"But it's safe?"

The receptionist frowned. "You know, to be on the safe side?"

"I don't understand," Evelyn said, feeling as if they'd beamed her into an episode of *The Twilight Zone* where words had disconnected from their meanings. "If it's safe, I must be on the safe side, right?"

The receptionist smiled sympathetically. "Of course. Take a seat."

Evelyn sat down and tried to shrug off everyone's concern by furiously researching the scientific consensus on MRIs during pregnancy, which she'd already done—five times. There is no evidence that MRIs harm either mother or baby, and it has been significantly researched.

Reassured, she took a few deep breaths and tried to relax, which was difficult because she could feel another migraine coming on.

Soon, a young doctor with brown hair, middle parted, entered the waiting room. The receptionist rushed up from her chair and, covering her mouth, said "She's pregnant" in what she thought was a whisper but—Evelyn assured me, emphatically—wasn't.

The doctor gestured for Evelyn to follow him. They sat down in his office. "I see you're pregnant," he said. "Are you sure you want to do the MRI?"

"Yes," she said. "Because I'm having bad migraines."

"I see," he said, which wasn't the same thing as being convinced by what he saw. "So, you *don't* want to wait then? Just to be on the sa—"

"No," she said. "Just do it already."

It's easy for pregnant women—encouraged to play safe by the medical industry, shouted at by Global Baby Defenders, and given endless advice by well-meaning friends and strangers—to become trapped in a default *don't* world. Where all risk is too much risk. Where the old line about "absence of evidence is not evidence of absence" is taken too seriously. Where there's a lot of talk about juries, and how they're still out.

People love sides, love to split everything into good and bad, black and white, safe and unsafe, but life abhors sides; it has only gradients. In order to get to each of these concerned medical professionals, Evelyn walked up and down fourteen flights of stairs, crossed fifteen roads full of speeding cars, took six escalators and four elevators, and rode in two trains.

There is no safe side. There is just less safe and safer. Acceptable risk and unacceptable risk. But there's always risk. Life is a death sentence.

Your job is to help her navigate this overly cautious, safe-side world. To not let it shrink her life down to just the walls inside your home. Don't join in the policing of her body. Instead, police the policing of her body. Because some half million years after *Homo heidelbergensis*, if the jury is still out on something, the jury is irrelevant.

Default *do*. Don't default *don't*.

Who Are You Again?

Evelyn was on the couch propped up by a dozen cushions, as always. I sidled up next to her.

"What do you want?" she asked.

"For you to make some space so I can lie down next to you."

"Do I have to?"

"Err... yes?"

"Fine," she said, wriggling slightly towards the wall, creating fifty centimetres for me to slip into. I lay down, sort of, just about, and then leaned over for a quick peck on the—

"DON'T," she barked.

I froze, lips puckered.

"I'm sorry," she said, "but I just find the idea of kissing you ridiculous."

"Oh," I said. "Right."

She let out a villainous laugh.

"What are you laughing at?"

"Kissing," she said, as if it were a faraway place we'd never been to. As if it were Mogadishu. Or *Mogakissu*.

"When did we last touch?" I asked. "Or cuddle?"

"Your unborn child touches me all the time. *Inside.* Isn't that enough? And we're touching right now, aren't we?"

"Yeah, but only because you haven't given me any space. My ass is hanging off the couch."

"You have plenty of space," she said.

I tried to turn onto my back but tumbled onto the floor. "Ow," I said. "That was my favourite hip." I waited for laughter. There was no laughter. We'd once found each other riotously funny. The couch she was hogging was the same couch that had so dominated the first year of our relationship. We only ever left it in stages of undress, climbing over piles of frenetically discarded clothes to get more wine. We would kiss for hours, eyes locked, stopping only to gush the stories of our lives at each other. Always, we touched. This woman—the greatest, smartest, kindest, sexiest I had ever known—couldn't get enough of me back then. The only thing she'd found "ridiculous" was being apart.

What had happened to us? What had happened to her? I looked up at her from the hard, wooden floor and thought, *Who are you again?*

You will almost certainly be noticing significant changes in your partner. Perhaps they're as unrecognisable to you as Evelyn was to me. They might want more affection and reassurance. They might want none. Feeling the pressure of impending motherhood, a person with a brilliant, sharp mind—someone who once spent sixteen hours researching tumble dryers and who had Excel spreadsheets of her Excel spreadsheets—might become a wild, unknown thing completely willing to restrict herself from eating Haribo for six months just because of a casual comment her friend Angela made about her friend Jill who had a friend Janet who ate a jumbo pack of fizzy strawberries and got pregnancy diabetes.

Who knows? The pregnancy spectrum is wide. The crap-shoot is deep.

And anyway, you're changing too, as we've already discussed. It's just easier for you to notice her changes because you have distance from her and you're all bunched up inside of yourself. But the changes are there. You're being primed for fatherhood. Your testosterone lowered. Your desire to nest heightened, even if there's no one in that nest who wants to cuddle with you yet.

She's not the only one gaining weight, either, is she? Men gain an average of 6.3 kilograms (14 pounds) during their partner's pregnancy[1], either from sympathetic snacking or because their cortisol has shot up too. An increase in cortisol will make it feel as if you're in a battle, which will make you think you're ravenously hungry, which will make you crave peanut butter straight from the tub.

She swings from sated to HANGRY in a single minute. She's started stashing snacks everywhere and then forgetting where she's put them, like a squirrel with amnesia. Remember last week, when you were on that walk and she found a snack stashed in her coat's inside pocket?

Rarely have you seen someone that happy. Her eyes cart-wheeled.

No, you admit, she's no longer the person you once knew, but that's exciting too, isn't it? Like getting a new girlfriend every week. And anyway, change is life's only constant. A point that parenting is really going to hammer home, you're sure. For to have a child is to sit in change's front row with an unobstructed view of all its delicious losses and gains.

Soon you two will have a newborn baby, but even that won't last long. You'll blink a few times. Fight a few times. Nap a few times. And then boom: it'll just be a baby. That won't last long, either. Blink. Fight. Nap. Boom: toddler. Blink. Fight. Nap. Child. Preteen. Teen. Suddenly—the days long but the decades short—you'll find yourself fighting over sofa space with your nearly grown child. They'll push you to the floor and you'll bash your favourite hip and look up at them as they stare down at you, now old. And you'll both be thinking the same thing: *Who are you again?*

The Quickening

"Ooooh," Evelyn said, as we lay side by side in our newly purchased Emperor King Bling Warlord bed—eight metres by eight metres. Her idea. We really wouldn't have to touch ever again.

"What?" I asked, rubbing my hands over the dark-blue sheets, once pirate-ship sails.

"It just kicked me. Well, it felt more like a flutter. I don't think it's very strong yet. And its feet are probably the size of acorns."

"Good on him/her," I said, and stretched as far as I could to reach for Evelyn's hand or arm or hip or whatever. "It's really happening, this baby thing."

"It's really happening," she said, and wriggled over, taking my hand and putting it on her bump. "Can you feel it?"

I focused all my attention. "No," I said, a minute later.

"Soon," Evelyn said. "Hey, if you want, every time it kicks me, I could kick you? Like sympathy kicks? Very couvade, no?"

"You'd never reach me in this bed."

"The quickening," she said.

"What?"

"When you feel the baby for the first time."

"Shouldn't it be called the thickening, or the prickling, or the tickling, or the… kickaling?"

She wrinkled her nose. "It's an Old English term. I think it means *alive*, or something like that. It was in one of the books."

We lay silent for a while. I tried to picture a miniature mix of her and me, physically so opposite, bunched up in a ball in Evelyn's belly making tiny kicks with nubby acorn feet. It was hard work. "It's really happening," I said again, anyway, even though I still didn't believe it.

She took my hand off the bump, wrapped it in hers, and squeezed. The intimacy was thrilling. My heart rate sped up. We hadn't been this physically entwined in months.

"I'm happy we're going to have this experience," she said.

"Can we kiss?" I asked, scrambling closer before this unicorn of a moment galloped away.

Her villainous laugh returned. "Kissing."

The Sex

We were in the waiting room of Evelyn's gynaecologist. COVID-19 numbers were down, so I'd be allowed in the room for the twenty-week "abnormality" scan. We were about to learn the sex of the baby, one of the structural walls in the house of personhood. It was thrilling, sitting there in our masks, our glasses fogging up as we breathed.

"My boss is having a girl," she said. "Just found out yesterday."

"Did she want a girl?"

Evelyn nodded. "She's thrilled, even said, 'Although we don't say it, deep down we all want girls.'"

We laughed because we both wanted a girl. Not, like, a lot more. Just a bit. The mildest of mild preferences. I can't even say why, exactly, only that perhaps the idea of raising a boy felt slightly less interesting. That if you taught him a few manners, to listen as much as he talked, and to respect women as his equal, he'd automatically be one of the good ones. Raising a strong, confident, liberated woman seemed like a thornier challenge. Also, having experienced puberty as a male, I just couldn't wish that level of horniness on anyone.

They called us in. Evelyn lay down, as she had in so many rooms like this during the time we'd spent trying to become pregnant. The doctor gestured me towards a small white stool. The equipment had a distinctly 1990s vibe. I had hoped for one of the new 4-D scans. Would have happily paid extra for one, even, because I'd read in one of the daddy books that men reported feeling more bonded to the baby after them.

An image flashed up on the screen. I gasped. Even with this ancient technology, I could make out way more than during the twelve-week scan. There was now a discernible head, arms, and legs.

Watching it, I felt a great sharp shock of... something. The feeling was hard to define, but I appreciated how much of it there was compared to the last scan.

Awe?

Pride?

My chest swelled. I wiped away a tear. I did not deserve this. No one deserved this. A person. A whole person. For us.

Evelyn dabbed her eyes, her mascara running.

"Do you want to know the sex?" the gynaecologist asked.

We nodded softly.

"A girl," she said, moving the wand back and forth over the same spot, taking photos, zooming in. "Lovely head," she said. "She's healthy."

She.

Her.

Never again would it be an *it*. We sobbed and kissed through our masks. If kissing was "ridiculous" before, masks didn't really help.

· · ·

As you push deeper into the second trimester, you will face the same decision we did—do you want to know the sex?

It's one of the more fun prebirth debates because, ultimately, the stakes aren't very high. It's not like picking a wrong name and damning your child to decades of bullying. You're just choosing between knowing something earlier or later. Earlier usually means in this scan, often called the anomaly scan, which is done somewhere between weeks eighteen and twenty. In theory, you could find out much sooner, from blood tests (as early as week eight, but they're more reliable the later they're done). This scan might also be done as part of certain genetic-disorder tests:

- Chorionic villus sampling
- Amniocentesis (where samples of the placenta or amniotic fluid are taken for testing)
- Non-invasive prenatal tests

But these aren't standard. Ultimately, most couples do elect to know. It's hard to get reliable figures, but one study from 2012 found that 69 percent of pregnant women and 77 percent of their partners wanted to know the sex of the foetus[1]. Apparently, the trend is now swinging back in the other direction, towards mystery. Perhaps, because the process of pregnancy is so medicalised, people want to keep one last surprise?

The advantage of knowing is that you halve the naming work and it might make it easier to imagine the baby, which might strengthen the bond you feel with it. It's also a good excuse for a party, and more parties are better than fewer, right?

But by not knowing, by keeping that surprise, you'll stop people from gender colour-coding every gift they give you:

blue for boys, pink for girls. And more surprises are better than fewer, right?

Tricky.

Once you know, you can't un-know. So, if you're on the fence, it's probably better to choose not to. You're then free to change your mind at any point during the rest of the pregnancy. Or you might find out by accident, even. Some friends of ours who'd wanted to be surprised found it written on documents given to them after the twenty-week scan.

If you choose to know, you don't have to worry much about the accuracy of the prediction. They might not give a prediction during the scan, if the baby's positioning is wrong, but if they do, studies show they're overwhelmingly accurate (in one study, 100 percent accurate and they could make a prediction 97 percent of the time[2]).

She's Viable

I was at my desk polishing an already gleaming sentence.

"Do you know what today is?" Evelyn asked.

I looked up. She was wearing her special pregnancy jeans with the wide band of elastic around the top.

"Sunday," I said.

She lowered her head. "It's Monday, honey."

"Oh, right. *Fine.*" Days mean little to the self-employed. "Is it an important Monday?"

"The app says yes." She had a pregnancy app on her phone, and we viewed it together on the weekends, seeing what was new, zooming in to admire the baby's new fingernails or a new schlock of head hair. We must have forgotten to check it this weekend. "She's viable, it says."

"If she came out now, she'd survive?"

She nodded. "Viable. Our daughter. Just about."

I leaned back in my chair, clasping my hands behind my head. "That's quite a thing to know."

We shared a silent, golden, awe-splashed moment of mutual reverie until… "Ice cream?" she asked.

"You read my mind."

Pop Culture Lies

By now, from all your research, you'll have likely realised that popular culture—that idiot megaphone, that pervasive peddler of partial truths, wild anecdotes, junk science, and fruity ancient wisdom—has spread a lot of misinformation about pregnancy and birth. At the end of the second trimester, past the midpoint to parenthood, let's check how ready you are with a quick quiz.

It's one point for each correct answer. To pass, you have to get at least eight points.

Q1. A pregnancy is how many months?

A: Nine months, stupid. Everyone knows a pregnancy is nine months.
B: Ten months.
C: Four and a half months.

* * *

Almost everyone on earth thinks a pregnancy is nine months. But it's ten months (forty weeks). The time until the missed period is counted, which is usually a month. So, the answer is *B*.

Q2. You're cuddled up on the sofa watching *Game of the Ring of the Power of the Throne* when your partner clutches her throat and runs to the bathroom. That's weird, because morning sickness happens...

A: In the morning. I can't even believe you're asking me this question.
B: Anytime.
C: Never. It's a myth.

* * *

Morning sickness, despite the name, can happen at any time of the day and is very common, affecting 70 to 80 percent of pregnant women, mostly in the first trimester.[1] *B* again.

Q3. You're dining out at a tragically hip urban restaurant where all the servers look as if they've fallen off a swimwear calendar. Everywhere you look, there are fringes straighter than rulers. Your partner keeps the server away because she's still researching on her phone what she can order. Pregnant women have to be careful when it comes to...

A: Eating seafood.
B: Eating raw and spicy food.
C: Worrying too much about what they eat.

* * *

The evidence for avoiding any food during pregnancy is pretty shaky. Certain foods can increase the risk of some illnesses, sure, but even with the increased risk, the decision to eat it would fall into most people's acceptable range. That said, high-mercury seafood is easy to avoid, and it's probably worth doing so. High-omega-3 seafood, however, such as salmon and shrimp, is great for foetal brain development. As for spicy food, well, India is a pretty populous place, so I think you can draw your own conclusions about the effects of spice on pregnancy. It also does nothing to induce labour. That's another myth. C.

4. You go to the cupboard but the cupboard is bare, again. The mum-to-be in your house has adopted a very clear *no snacks left behind* policy. While pregnant, she needs to eat...

A: For about one and a third.
B: For two. *Yay.*
C: As she would normally eat.

* * *

She should eat want she wants, as always, but if we're talking purely about calories as opposed to comfort food, your growing child needs only about three hundred to five hundred extra calories per day. *A.*

5. While pregnant, your partner is most likely to...

A: Crave the same sort of food as a late-night stoner.

B: Crave chocolate.
C: Crave pickles with ice cream and other baffling food combinations.

* * *

While some women crave random combinations of food, these cravings are nowhere near as prevalent as they appear to be in the movies. It's more likely she'll crave highly specific foods, a sign she's deficient in that nutrient, or just calorie-dense foods such as bread and pasta. The biggest change won't be how much she eats but the speed with which she races from content to hangry. If you want a peaceful life, up your snack game. *A.*

6. The sex of your child is decided by...

A: The whims of the gods.
B: The whims of the woman's genes.
C: The whims of the man's sperm.

* * *

We now know that all those queens punished for not producing male heirs were badly wronged. Eggs are always X chromosome, while sperm can be X or Y, so it's the sperm that decide the baby's gender. *C.*

7. Because of all those delicious hormonal changes, pregnant women...

A: Glow like happy suns, radiating oxytocin.

B: Dim like sad pandas.
C: Relive their teenage years—in other words, they get acne and/or blotchy or dry skin.

* * *

While some women experience a healthy glow due to increased blood flow, changes to the skin are more common. *C.*

8. The pregnant woman who just ran past you in the park is...

A: Living her life and wants you to mind your own business.
B: Taking a big risk.
C: Running straight to the hospital to give birth.

* * *

While each woman should listen to her body and not exercise through pain, the pregnant body is very capable and benefits from exercise, just as every other body. *A.*

9. Birth starts when...

A: She pops like a water balloon, gushing water everywhere, and screams, "The baby's coming! The baby's coming!"
B: She dilates to over eight centimetres.
C: She has persistent contractions.

* * *

On TV, every birth begins with water breaking, but this is actually pretty uncommon. Only 8–10 percent of people have their water break before labour begins[2]. There will probably be a few false starts—times when contractions begin then end—so it's hard to know for sure when *this is really it*. There are three stages of birth: the dilation stage, the expulsion stage, and the placental stage. If contractions persist and strengthen, and the gaps between them shorten, the first stage of labour has begun. C.

10. The contractions are every few minutes now and you're in a taxi, speeding towards the hospital. Disaster. It's the FIFA World Cup final today. You'd love to watch it, or at least follow along on your phone. The kickoff is in six hours. That's plenty of time, right?

A: It's unlikely, but if you're lucky, or it goes to penalties, you might see a bit.
B: No chance, sunshine.
C: For sure, it's going to be fine. Births are notoriously fast.

* * *

Get your head in the game, man. And no, not that game. On TV, the woman lies down, screams, pants ten times, and then the baby falls out. In real life? No. Just no. The average first-time birth is fourteen hours. Turn off your phone already. *B*.

11. You're at the hospital and they've finally let you into the birthing room. As well as a bed, there's a pool and a birthing chair and some kinky bondage straps. Why? Women give birth...

A: Squatting or standing.
B: Lying on their back.
C: Lying on their front.

* * *

No matter what TV has told you, she's very unlikely to be flat in the bed, legs spread, pushing. They just do this in the movies because it's easy to film, most take the supine position only very late in labour. The answer is *A*.

12. The kid is out, thank god. That was the worst, longest, most stressful night of your life, and you didn't even do the work. Speaking of which, they've just put some scissors in your hand. You have to cut the umbilical cord...

A: A few minutes after birth.
B: Straight away, chop-chop.
C: After half an hour and a strong coffee.

* * *

It used to be *B*, but we now know there's a benefit to waiting a few minutes, so those last drops of blood and oxygen can flow from placenta to child. This also gives you time to stare, shocked and confused, at this weird, smudged, crusty lump that people are telling you is your child, and to reassure your partner that yes, the birth really, really is over, and that she did fantastically well. *A*.

Part Three
The Third Trimester
The Final Countdown

What Happens When Again?

You're nearly there. You're nearly there. You're nearly there. It might not always feel that way. She might want to be much nearer there. But, really, you're nearly there. Let's take a look at the key developments in the third trimester.

Third trimester: Cloudy with a certainty of miserable

Mother: That giant blimp of a baby will put pressure on her organs, leading to heartburn, indigestion, shortness of breath, and all-day, every-day, garden-variety misery.

Go easy on her. You'd be miserable too.

Towards the end of this trimester, Braxton Hicks (i.e. practice) contractions begin, helping prepare the uterus for labour. By this point, she's probably desperate for it to just be over, while you might be at your most nervous and protective of your current lifestyle and freedoms. This is a disconnect you both need to manage closely. Make this trimester about her needs, not yours.

By week thirty-six, the baby's head will likely be moving

down into the pelvis in preparation for birth. You will need to have a lot of patience because it's unlikely she'll have much of it left.

Baby: By weeks twenty-five to twenty-eight, its lungs begin to work. It may even start to practice breathing by inhaling and exhaling amniotic fluid. Its eyes have improved too, and it can distinguish between light and dark. It's about the size of a cantaloupe.

By weeks twenty-nine to thirty-two, it's pretty much fully developed and practising for life outside the womb. It has a sleep-wake cycle. It can suck and swallow. It's the size of a honeydew melon.

It will spend weeks thirty-three to thirty-six developing its fat stores, priming itself for life after birth. Oh, and it can hiccup now, too. You'll probably be able to hear it. And see it moving. It's pretty weird. You should also be regularly talking to it now. It'll be the size of a pineapple, although less spiky.

Your love is about to bear fruit. *Hurrah.*

This trimester is all about making the final preparations for your home and mind. Are you ready?

Let's find out.

Have the Conversation(s)

Becoming a parent is one of the few transformational events in life—unlike puberty, first love, heartbreak, death of a parent, etc.—that we're given a specific due date for. That's part of what makes this last trimester so special. You're in the *before* staring hard at the *after*—at the dissolution of *I* and the forging of a *We* in the fires of family.

Use these last few months to reflect on what type of father you want to be, and what sort of family you'll build with your partner. You'd be surprised how few people do this. It's easier to stumble forward, assuming you're on the same page about everything, living your life day by day in the micro, rather than pulling back and appraising your lives and love from a great height.

Why rock the boat?

Why hunt for incompatibility?

You must, my friend. An enormous relationship test is coming. Here are just a few things you might want to discuss beforehand:

- What do you want to do differently from your parents?

- What do you want to do differently from your peer group?
- Who are your parenting role models? Why?
- What about parenting do you expect to come easily to you? What do you think will be hard?
- What most excites you about taking this adventure with your partner?
- If you live together, how do you currently divide household tasks? (You might think it's fifty-fifty until you write them all down.) Now, estimate how much time they take. When it's revealed one of you is doing more, and it will be, are you going to be okay with that?
- How do you want to divide up parenting's many additional tasks? Is fifty-fifty the goal? How will you monitor that?
- At what age will you hire childcare or send Bebe to kindergarten?
- How will you share the family's money?
- How will you know if you're succeeding as parents? (More on this later.)
- And what about as lovers who are also parents?
- Do you want to establish regular check-in/feedback sessions to discuss how your relationship/parenting is going? How about weekly, on Sundays, when the baby's napping?

It's vital to have these conversations now, while you both have the time and space to resolve issues. You need to understand each other's deep-seated desires, fears, hopes, values, and stressors. It's what, in the hard, early years of parenting, will make you less likely to mistake your partner's fears for frustration, tiredness for anger, naivety for stupidity, forgetfulness for disinterest, and lack of energy for lack of love.

Define Success

In my midtwenties, after writing a couple of mediocre blog posts, I blagged my way into an interview at a startup. Despite the worst performance at a brain teaser (more of a brain torture) in human history, I was hired for an Internet-marketing position.

In my first months, I kept expecting my boss and colleagues to notice my flagrant ineptitude, fire me, then begin a thorough review of hiring practices. This would lead to more firings and perhaps also the swift implosion of the entire company and/or the universe.

For some reason, that never happened.

Instead, they gave me the task of creating a seasonal website, and somehow, more through luck than judgement, I managed to. It was held together by spit, sticky tape, and prayer. Only a few people liked it, and absolutely everyone else detested it, but the important thing, I felt, was that they could go to this website and form an opinion about it—it was online.

Then came the weekly team meeting. My colleague, Christian, raised concerns about the project and whether the (overwhelmingly hostile) response to it justified the (enormous) financial investment in it.

"It's a success," I said. "It's online."

"It doesn't work properly and everyone hates it."

"It's online," I repeated, because he still wasn't getting it. "It's a success. We can move on."

"Did we define success for this project?" he asked. "Then we'd have metrics to compare it against." He then said some other things, but I didn't hear them because my blood was boiling too loudly.

I've had about ten years to reflect on what Christian— whom I still take a moment to curse, each day, with a plague of hungry locusts—said in that meeting. I suppose I can see now, with the anaesthetising effect of time, that his approach had merit. That it was, in fact, that rarely spotted thing: the correct approach.

If you haven't defined success, it's difficult to know if you've achieved it. Of course, it's also easy to stand in the judgement of others, as Christian Craphead did. To hold them to higher standards than you might hold yourself.

Parenting is no different, of course.

I have a friend whose anonymity I will protect by saying only that her name rhymes with Smeverly. She has three daughters who... how can I put this delicately... are very young for their age. The oldest is eleven going on nine, the nine-year-old acts six, and the six-year-old acts three. None of them have ever worn shoes with shoelaces. They still get their food cut up for them. They still believe in the Easter Bunny.

I like Smeverly, but I've always judged her parenting. One day, I was at her house for dinner. After a frenetic, nerve-testing meal, as we cleared the table, which her undomesticated, wildling children had sprayed with half-digested chicken nuggets, I held an intervention.

"So," I said, probably while pretending to yawn. "Parenting. Difficult, right? Or not? Hard to say. Unless. Well. Did you ever define parenting success for yourself?"

She put down the plastic Frozen plates she was stacking. "That's a strange question."

I leaned back. "Is it?"

"Sort of out of the blue."

"Hmm," I said, looking up over her shoulder into the middle distance, which was, unfortunately, blocked by the fridge covered in the awful drawings of her cack-handed children. "Perhaps."

She looked down at the table, taking a moment to collect her thoughts. "Keeping them young and carefree," she said. "Childhood is such a special, magical time, you know? It's so unique to the human experience, so free of obligation, anxiety, and stress. I think we have to protect it at all costs."

"Oh," I said. "Right."

She picked up the plates and carried them through to the kitchen. I whistled to call off my attack dogs. No intervention was necessary. She was succeeding at parenting, as she'd defined it. I didn't agree with that definition, but once I knew it, her parenting choices made sense to me.

Her children will have a long time to be adults, but a very short shot at childhood. Smeverly was a happy child until puberty, when she developed chronic anxiety. She doesn't enjoy being an adult. She doesn't really seem to enjoy anything much, other than maybe her children. Or, more specifically, as I now know, her children being children.

Much of parenting is reacting in the heat of the moment, fighting micro fires. It's very hard to get the time, space, and energy to evaluate how you're doing on a macro level. That's why now matters. Identify the North Star that will guide you during all the really hard decisions coming your way.

Evelyn and I didn't do this before she was pregnant. I

wish we'd thought to. It would have been a good way for us to see if we wanted the same things. If we had compatible values. By the time we did finally have the conversation, we were deep into the third trimester and sitting out on the balcony having dinner on our laps. Evelyn was the cook in our household, but late-stage pregnancy had changed things. I'd stepped up and felt that, despite abandoning the recipe and using only half the ingredients, my first-ever soup had been a great success.

"How will we know if we did a good job?" I asked. "As parents. What's success for you?"

She blinked several times. "I think our job is to make ourselves redundant."

I smiled. "Yes," I said. "Exactly. Our job is to prepare them as best we can for this world, then get out of their way." I ladled another delicious spoonful of pumpkin soup into my mouth, feeling smug about the partner I'd picked.

"This soup," she said. "Did you taste it while you were making it?"

"No."

"It's just water."

I tipped my bowl ever so slightly towards her and ran my spoon lazily through the pale-orange liquid to show her how smooth it was. "It's a success," I said. "It's a soup."

The One Thing

If your partner hates being fussed over, like Evelyn, you might become disillusioned, believing there's nothing you can offer during pregnancy.

It was late in the third trimester when I realised that there was actually something she wanted, even though she'd never expressed it in words. I now believe it's the one thing every pregnant person wants—and needs.

Every pregnant person wants and needs to know that no matter what's coming—no matter how deep you both fall into the parenting trenches, how sleep-deprived you are as you microwave milk at 3am, how many thousand times you sing "Twinkle, twinkle" while silently rocking and begging your baby to go back to sleep and fantasising about fleeing to Abu Dhabi to become a golf instructor for oligarchs—you will stay with her, with your child, and do the work.

The crappy, tedious, unglamorous labour of putting someone else's needs in front of your own, day after day, with minimal thanks, praise, or acknowledgement.

That feeling, that safety, that security, that certainty: it's priceless. Give it to her.

Parenting Styles

With success defined and an agreed goal in mind, both of you must decide on the best parenting style to reach it. You don't have to start from scratch, of course. There are many enticing pedagogic templates to adopt. Here's an overview of ten popular styles.

1. Authoritative

Authoritative parents provide a clear framework for what's right and wrong, but they're not rigid—they're willing to be negotiated with. They know best only until they're shown otherwise. They don't use fear, demands, or punishment and instead let consequences guide behaviour. They try to ask more than tell.

In practice: "The other day it was snowing, and little Timmy pulled off his gloves on the way to kindergarten, even though he'd seen me struggle to put them on his hands. I stopped and told him why it was so important to wear them (because we lose our heat from our extremities). Looking around, I pointed out that everyone else was wearing gloves, and then I told him that if he didn't, he'd get a cold and then we wouldn't be able to go to Trampoline World at the weekend. Eventually, he put the gloves back on."

Pro: Can promote self-esteem and good decision-making if authority is enforced consistently. It allows children to question with the knowledge that there's a line that cannot be crossed.

Con: Can be time-consuming for parents to have to explain their position on every issue, and then have that position be interrogated.

Pop-culture parent: Jack (and Rebecca) Pearson, from *This Is Us.*

Likely therapy costs: Low

2. Authoritarian

Authoritarian parents knows best. Or maybe loudest. These parents aren't to be messed with. They're overseers with strict rules and high expectations. Where they lead, their children subserviently follow.

In practice: "When he took the gloves off? I stopped the bike and told him that if he liked the cold so much, he could take the rest of his clothes off as well. His teeth were chattering pretty hard when we got to school. I let him keep his underwear on, though, which was more than my father would have allowed. He now puts his own gloves on each morning, and mine too, which tells you all you need to know, doesn't it?"

Pro: Drill-sergeant parents can provide needed structure and discipline provided that their rules are clear, logical, and consistently enforced.

Cons: Acting as if a child's wishes and opinions don't matter is a quick way to convince them that their wishes and opinions don't matter—never good for the ol' self-esteem. Also, the narrower and more rigid their world, the quicker they're forced to bump against its edges, which can earn them the label "rebellious", which will make the authoritarian parent narrow their world further. The child will then inevitably overstep, and a depressing discipline arms race will begin.

Pop-culture parent: Miranda Priestly, from *The Devil Wears Prada.*

Likely therapy costs: High

3. Permissive

Permissive parents don't ask why. They ask why not. If something won't harm the child, they're going to allow it. Yeah, the kids in class love to come over to Permissive Parent's house because every bed is a bouncy castle, it's always popcorn for dinner, and the only thing no is said to is common sense.
In practice: "The glove thing? What a lark. I took mine off as well. It was less funny when the frostbite kicked in. We cried together. Are thumbs important?"

Pro: MEGA FUN.

Con: Having never met a gratification they needed to delay, permissive parents' children may develop a severe case of compulsiveness and a disrespect of authority. This can cause violent clashes with the wider world—which tends to be stiff, unforgiving, and kind of a killjoy.

Pop-culture parent: Peter Griffin, from *Family Guy.*

Likely therapy costs: Medium

4. Attachment

Parents who use this style are aiming to develop a strong emotional bond with their child. It's characterised by gentle discipline, high emotional availability, strong empathy, and lots of cuddling.

In practice: "'What's that all about, honey?' I said, stopping the bike after Timmy threw the gloves down. 'Don't know,' he replied. I picked up the glove and put it back on his hand. He took it off. I put it on. He took it off. 'This is fun, isn't it?' I said. 'You've made a game. Good job. I love you. You're so creative.' He started crying. 'Do you not want to go to kindergarten?' I asked. 'Is that what all this is really about?' He picked his nose. 'I thought so,' I said. 'Well, okay, how about we go back home and cuddle up on the sofa and watch cartoons instead?' He nodded. 'I love you,' I said. 'Never leave me.'"

Pro: When done right, this type of parenting can help foster emotional intelligence and a resilient child who knows their parents will always have their back (and front and sides).

Con: When done badly, attachment parents become overprotective, and perhaps even more codependent than their child, who, as they age, will feel as if they're the parent in the relationship.

Pop-culture parent: Lorelai Gilmore, from *Gilmore Girls*

Likely therapy costs: Medium

5. Uninvolved

Uninvolved parents offer their children little emotional support or guidance because they're busy with their own lives, were the children of hands-off parents themselves, or think this is the best way to raise an independent child.
In practice: "Kindergarten? Oh, so that's where they go all day? Huh. Wait, who gave him gloves?"

Pro: Both parent and child get a lot of time to explore their own interests.

Con: Those interests might be detrimental, dangerous, or both (e.g. fireworks). The world is confusing, and unless role models step in to explain it, children can get very lost.

Pop-culture parent: Homer Simpson, from *The Simpsons.*

Likely therapy costs: Medium

6. Free-range

Free-range parenting allows children autonomy and self-directed exploration. The world is as much the teacher as the caregiver is, and how kids get to the answers matters as much as the answers themselves. Free-range parents won't stop their kids from doing something a little risky—they'll go get the bandages ready.

In practice: "I could tell he regretted taking off his gloves when he started crying. I stopped the bike. 'Cold hands, huh?' I said. His teeth were chattering too much to answer. 'That's why I wear gloves,' I said, demonstrating mine. There was silence. 'Where are yours?' He shrugged. 'Shame,' I said, blowing on his hands to warm them up. I got back on the bike and pedalled twice as fast, so he'd be indoors quicker."

Pro: Can promote creativity and independence.

Con: May not provide enough structure or protection for more introverted children.

Pop-culture parent: Marmee March, from *Little Women.*

Likely therapy costs: Low

7. Helicopter

Helicopter parents buzz overhead, closely monitoring their progeny, always ready to swoop in and save them from any heartache, mistake, or minor decision (e.g. which crayon to draw with—*blue, the answer is blue*).

In practice: "Do you know how dangerous it is to bike in the snow? I wouldn't expose little Timmy to those kinds of risks. No, we took a taxi to school. I had to tell the driver to slow down a few times because it was too bumpy for me to do Timmy's homework, but we got there on time. I carried him in, just to be safe. Everyone was glad to see him, I know, because I gave him sweets to hand out."

Pro: Highly involved in their children's lives and decisions.

Con: Highly involved in their children's lives and decisions. With helicopter parents, it's hard to tell where the love ends and the micromanaging begins.

Pop-culture parent: Beverly Goldberg, from *The Goldbergs.*

Likely therapy costs: Medium

8. Lawnmower

While helicopter parents hover overhead, ready to swoop in when a problem arrives, lawnmower parents are even more proactive. They're not above, watching and waiting, they're on the ground, out in front of their children, rushing to clear all possible problems away before the child has even encountered them.

In practice: "Was it snowing? I don't think Timmy even noticed. The bubble he's sealed inside of is temperature controlled, you see. No, he doesn't go to school. Too much riff-raff. And anyway, he's perfectly happy here. I make sure of it. And he has plenty of friends, which are much cheaper than you'd imagine at their age. Far cheaper than a sibling."

Pro: These parents are very hands on, involved in their children's lives, and their children will feel that love intensely.

Con: It's hard to develop resilience and problem-solving skills when nothing ever goes wrong. Children of these parents may develop the false belief they're the absolute centre of the universe, when really, it's only the parents' universe.

Pop-culture parent: Chris Traeger, from *Parks and Recreation*.

Likely therapy costs: High

9. Gentle

Gentle parenting is about building a nurturing, respectful, trusting relationship in which empathy and positive reinforcement are emphasised.

In practice: "I stopped the bike and explained the concept of hand warmth and blood flow to Timmy. He doubled down, so I backed off. His hands, his choice. I think, in the end, the blizzard was stronger than he expected and the frostbite more painful. I stopped the bike again when he started crying. 'What sweets should we buy after school?' I asked. While he was distracted deciding between Smarties and Skittles, I slipped the gloves back on his hands."

Pro: While this approach can be good for emotional regulation, it's easy for these parents to be *too* gentle in areas they don't realise are important until it's too late.

Con: The world will never be as gentle as these parents, yet their kids will have to learn to navigate it anyway.

Pop-culture parent: Bob Belcher, from *Bob's Burgers*.

Likely therapy costs: Low

10. Tiger

Fodder for many an immigrant memoir, the tiger parent emphasises high (usually impossibly so) achievement and strict discipline in the hope that their children will have a better life than they did.

In practice: "The glove thing? Such a disrespect. I told him how many houses I had to clean to buy those gloves for him, and how, when I was a kid, we had only one pair of gloves for the entire village. We dreamed of having our own set. He put on the gloves. I ripped them back off and threw them on the ground. 'Happy now?' I said. 'You don't deserve the gloves, anyway. Also, these gloves are my heart.' I stomped on them. Snow? That wasn't snow. That was nothing. Where I grew up, we had real blizzards, not the stupid slushy-ice weather they have here. Where did I grow up? Laos."

Pro: Learning the hard way is a skill in itself and can set a child on a path to success and achievement.

Con: Too much success and achievement too early makes little Timmy a dull boy who thinks the love of his parents is conditional on him becoming a nuclear physicist astronaut rocketpreneur.

Pop-culture parent: Amy Chua, from the film *The Joy Luck Club.*

Likely therapy costs: Medium

Stuff

How do you know a birth is imminent? You swim rather than walk through your home.

With a week to go, I front-crawled into the living room and found Evelyn surrounded by great piles of knick-knacks. A last-minute audit was occurring. As I passed, on my way to the balcony, she held up and then squeezed a small bulb-shaped object with a spout, dousing me as if she were one of those women in the perfume department.

Air came out.

Or went in.

Maybe both.

"What's that?" I asked.

"Robin gave it to us as a present."

"But what is it?"

"A nasal aspirator," she said, as if this were obvious.

"A nasal whatspirator?"

She squeezed it again. "It sucks the boogers out, basically."

I froze. There was a loud ripping sound that I knew immediately was the space-time continuum tearing in two. A great chasm opened beneath me and I tumbled in, my arms flailing.

Falling.

Falling.

Always falling.

Down became up. Up became down. Up and down became not the point. All became it. It became no.

I screamed.

No one heard.

I crashed, winded, on my back at the bottom of a deep well. It was cold and damp. I was afraid. From this dark, confusing place, I looked up at Evelyn, on our red couch. She was putting things into boxes and pulling them out, seemingly happy in this so-called Real World, living as if it still made sense there, as if it hadn't collapsed under the weight of its own absurdity.

I screamed.

No one heard.

A single phrase looped in my mind: *It sucks the boogers out, basically.*

I was down there for an inordinate amount of time.

I was down there for eternity.

I screamed.

No one heard.

I screamed.

No one heard.

I screamed.

Someone must have heard because a hand reached down for me. At the end of it was a nasal aspirator. It sucks the boogers out, basically. It sucked me up too and dropped me back into the living room. Thrilled to be back, I hugged myself all over.

"What are you doing?" Evelyn asked.

I let go of myself. "Nothing."

"Why did you say 'help'?"

"I just… well." I swept away baby-themed detritus and perched on the edge of the sofa. "You live to see thirty-eight," I said, "and you think, I'm a man who knows things, you know? It sucks the boogers out, basically. I mean… it's not great, the world, but I've made my peace with its excesses, its vulgarity, its waste, hubris, and flimflam." I turned and, with my eyes, pleaded, although I wasn't sure for what. "Now I know how deep the well goes."

She rolled her eyes and may have stopped listening.

"I think, I suppose," I continued, "that it sucks the boogers out, basically."

"Can you stop saying 'it sucks the boogers out, basically'?"

I tipped my head to the side and banged my ear several times. "I believe I can't, no. My mind had been blown by tat. Do you know the English word *tat*?" Evelyn was German, but you barely noticed, and anyway, no one's perfect. It sucks the boogers out.

Basically.

Her eyebrows smushed together. "No."

"How about the word *naff*?"

"Is this going somewhere?"

"This thing, this object"—I gestured to it—"this deboogerer. It's like the El Dorado of naff tat. Of tatnaff."

"It just sucks out boogers," she said, giving it another couple of pumps. "What's the problem?"

"That's it, I think. That's the nature of my quibble. Was there a problem to be solved?"

"Boogers?" she offered casually.

"Yes."

"It's hard for babies to breathe with boogers," she said. "Babies have tiny noses."

"Do they?" I said sarcastically. "I thought everything else about them was small except their full-size adult conks."

"Nah," she said.

"And so, it sucks the boogers out?"

"Basically."

"Are they not tiny boogers, though?" I pressed. "Commensurate with the nose that both births and houses them until this violent device rips them out? And did you and I not make it to adulthood fine with nothing to suck the boogers out basically? Or even expertly?"

She shrugged. "Maybe our parents had one?"

"They didn't, Ev. No, there is a real nasty waft of late capitalism about this."

"Yeah, but we also both have big noses."

"The kid will too."

"It just—"

I nodded. "Sucks the boogers out, basically."

She shoved it up her nose and squeezed. She grinned. "It's good. Tickles."

"Give me a go, then," I said, holding out my hand.

With the baby almost here, you should also be auditing. I understand there's a temptation to buy everything. To buy all of it. You want to be prepared. You want to show your love.

Restrain yourself, brother.

Those "Everything You Need for Your Baby" lists tend to be compiled by epic swindlers. They'd sell you their own mother for five bucks. (Actually, a mother for five bucks would be a tremendous bargain. Buy two.)

So, rather than give you a similarly comprehensive list, I'll just tell you the things that, in our experience (n = 1), you don't need. Or that we needed but purchased incorrectly because those lists of lies led us astray.

. . .

Not very important things you probably don't need at all:

1. Fancy newborn outfits. (Babies grow quickly and everyone gifts rompers, which are amazing and adults should wear too. You need a dozen of them.)
2. Toys. (Until your child is about a year old, anything can/will be a toy. As a general rule, if a dog would find it fascinating, your six-month-old will find it equally beguiling, e.g. a toilet-roll tube).
3. Baby shoes. (Would you buy gloves if you had no hands? Your baby doesn't know it has feet, and when it does, it will spend the first two months trying to eat them. It doesn't need shoes.)
4. Baby-specific dishes and utensils and a high chair. (Not needed until you introduce solid food.)
5. Books. (You have months to get these, and they're basically free at any flea market. Also, you'll get tons as gifts.)
6. Baby nail clippers or scissors. (Normal ones are fine if you don't cut while drunk.)
7. Baby towels and washcloths. (They have the same kind of body you have; they just have less of it.)
8. Milk-warming gizmo. (Most babies don't care about the temperature of their milk. This is a pointless task you can skip.)
9. Wet-wipe-warming gizmo. (Whoever invented this should be smothered to death in a pile of scorching-hot wet wipes).
10. NASA-approved diaper pail. (For a long time, we've known that trash stinks, so any regular bin with a sealable lid is going to do the job fine).
11. Twelve-pocketed super-fancy diaper bag. (Any complex system you create is just going to descend

faster into chaos. Just use a tote bag or something with a couple of pockets).

12. Fancy nursery decorations. (You know they can barely see, right? Their key sense in the beginning is smell. And just existing is exhausting for babies. It's going to sleep fine without a carousel of the cosmos.)

13. A baby bath. (Assuming you already have a bath, you can use that, or you can have a bath together, which is fun, or you can just use the sink).

Things we screwed up and you shouldn't

1. Too-low and too-heavy buggy/stroller. (You'll spend hundreds of hours of your life shoving this thing around, so your choice matters. For tall men, the most important thing is handle height. Your back will thank you for getting something with a high/adjustable bar (for the same reason, don't get a crib with sides you can't lower). The second key characteristic is weight. Can you lug it up and down a flight of stairs on your own? This matters enormously if you live in a major city with a subway system and the most finicky lifts in the modern world (hi, Berlin!). You don't need to buy a fancy buggy, or even a new one. Our replacement buggy (after I learned the painful way about the importance of handle height) was twenty-five euros second-hand, or maybe more like tenth-hand. It's amazing. I'll be sad when we have to give it up. I use it for everything, including the weekly shopping. Don't bend, or your body will break.)

2. Washable Diapers. (Researching whether to pick washable or disposable nappies was my task, and I really went to town on it. I lost several evenings comparing both systems, and even created a spreadsheet where I modelled upfront, ongoing, and long-time financial/CO_2 costs. Surprisingly, all my research suggested that there was no great environmental difference between them. It's hard to accept that, I know, because you can see disposable nappies stacking up and going into the bin and then the landfill, where they will sit, slowly decaying for about ten thousand years. Reusable nappies? They just go in the machine dirty, swirl around a bit, and come out clean, right? Nope. Wrong. You're not seeing the enormous material costs that went into creating them, and the energy costs of cleaning them. And you're underestimating how high the temperature of the water will have to be to get all that poop out (if you can get the poop out). And how often they'll leak, creating more cleaning and washing. I know several people who started with washables and abandoned them a month in. I know only one who made it the entire way through with them. Disposables almost never leak. They're amazing. I quietly deleted the spreadsheet. We don't talk about the spreadsheet.)

A general note about things

All the stuff you're excited about will end up being rubbish, and all the things you don't care about at all, that you buy on a whim for a shiny nickel, will be lifesaving. So it goes.

The best decision we made was joining what the young-sters are calling a "baby chain". Evelyn found it via the Sister-hood. This is where you find someone who has a child about three months older than yours and then get everything from them. Then you find someone three months behind you, and you pass everything on to them. Kids grow rapidly, far faster than they can wear out clothes and toys. Occasionally, you throw some money forward down the chain.

This arrangement saved us a fortune. Anything not provided by the chain we got at flea markets, which, in Berlin, are just giant mountains of kid stuff people desper-ately foist upon you as you pass, in exchange for loose change. They're just so happy to have it out of their house.

The Baby-Mindhog Effect

Evelyn stood at the edge of the playground, one hand gripping her elbow, a stance she often adopted when annoyed. I knelt deeper in the sandpit, running my hand through the coarse lumps. A bald baby in a blue romper with a duck on it stared up at me from over the edge of his bucket and spade, a sloppy yet cautious half-grin on his oval face.

"No glass in this one," I shouted to Evelyn. "So that's good. Cat poop, but that comes with the territory, I suppose."

"There's a sign warning about needles over here," she said.

"Hmm," I said, standing up, brushing sand from my trousers, and giving a brisk nod. "It's okay. I could imagine coming here with the kid, at a push. And it's only a six-minute walk. Update the spreadsheet. C plus."

"I'm not touching your spreadsheet."

I pulled out my phone. "I want to do another one before we head home."

She sucked in her lips, another classic gesture of the irritation genre. "This is irritating," she said, unnecessarily.

"There's a playground near that new hipster bakery," I

said, starting the timer app on my phone and striding past her.

"There's a playground there?" She hurried to keep step with me. "I never noticed."

I noted the heavily pregnant woman climbing out of the red car to our left, and the two children skipping unattended on the opposite side of the road, holding hands. It would have been cute if it weren't potentially deadly. A bicycle courier approached them at speed. I prepared to shout in warning. "I notice everything now," I said, as the courier saw them and slowed down. Peril avoided, for now. "ALL OF IT. Always."

"You're weird," she said. "How did I not notice before you got me pregnant?"

"Science got you pregnant," I said. "Don't try to pin that shit on me."

We walked to the other park. It was modest. Only one functional swing, a slide that lacked slippiness, and a poorly executed Arabian Nights theme for which the architect should have been publicly scorned then cancelled. I added it to the spreadsheet and gave it a D. On the way home, we stopped to buy a sourdough loaf that cost only slightly less than my four-year university education. On the way, I saw two more pregnant women, three newborns in strollers, and a seriously milk-drunk toddler.

"EVERY WOMAN ON EARTH IS PREGNANT," I said.

Evelyn laughed. "Have you heard of the Baader-Meinhof effect?"

"Yes," I lied. I subtly thumbed away from the timer app and googled *Baader-Meinhof effect*.

You might know the effect as the frequency illusion. The idea is that if you buy a red car, you'll notice every other red car on earth. Your brain is a master filter, and with billions of bits of information bombarding it, it has to pick what to focus on, or you'd be too overwhelmed to function. What does it choose? Whatever's on your mind, of course.

Before Evelyn was pregnant, all these waddling women, mediocre playgrounds, skipping children, and bald babies in blue rompers with ducks on them were irrelevant. Invisible. Even though children are absolutely everywhere—squawking, cartwheeling, enthusiastically freeloading, and hanging upside down off things looking for exciting new ways to hurt themselves.

As you enter the end of the third trimester, you'll likely find that your neighbourhood has transformed before your eyes, all its clinics, family centres, soft-play zones, playgrounds, toy stores, and cafés—where every surface is easy to wipe down and the default seat is a high chair—coming sharply into focus. It's like discovering a secret society operating in broad daylight, hidden under only a cloak of lameness. There's no secret handshake, and the admission policy is generous; anyone with a tiny human is welcome.

You will be a member soon. Until then, study them, research them, time the walking distance between their various social hangouts, and grade their facilities in a spreadsheet. You have no choice—the Baby-Mindhog effect has you in its clutches.

I'm Done

One week to go. Her curiosity about the experience is long gone and has been replaced with resentment against the duration and discomfort of it. She is enormous, seemingly as wide as she is tall, but still attractive to you, no matter how repulsive she finds herself.

She doesn't go out much anymore. Stairs take too much of a toll and anyway, she practically lives on the toilet. The only place you go together is the hospital. Every time you're out, people are impossibly kind. Cars brake from a block away and you have an automatic right to subway seats, café chairs, and prime pavement real estate. You jump every queue. You feel like minor royals.

It's nice, but it's not enough for her. "I'm done," she says, as you enter the hospital for yet another check-up.

"I know, honey."

"There just isn't enough space in me. And the damn kid wriggles all day. And the heartburn, my god, it's endless."

"That means the kid will be hairy, right?"

"She must be a damn yeti."

"Very active baby," the doctor says. "You're here so often you should have your own room."

"Tell me something I don't know," she replies.

She wants her body back.

She wants her life back.

Unfortunately, she won't get either for a long time yet.

You drive home in silence. "I'm so done," she says, panting and leaning over, as you root around for the door key.

"Any day now, my love."

The Secret Club

My friend Petra was sitting in a dark bar with her friend Tabby, a trainee midwife, and several of Tabby's colleagues. "Are you thinking of having kids one day?" Tabby asked.

"Yes," Petra said.

"No one will tell you the truth about birth."

All the women laughed.

"Tell me then."

"You sure you want to know?"

Petra considered it, took a breath, then nodded.

Tabby cracked her knuckles. "Birth is the worst thing imaginable. No one talks about it because there's no way of getting you ready for it, so no one even tries."

"But so many women have done it," Petra said.

"Yeah, because they didn't know what it was going to be like."

"But what about hypnobirthing, water births, orgasmic birth? Are there really no good births?"

"All monstrous, thundering lies," Tabby said, and her colleagues laughed harder. "There to guilt women so that when the birth is horrendous and traumatic, which it will be, which it always is, it'll be the woman's fault. It's always our fault."

Petra was quiet for a moment. "So, it's like a secret club?" she asked. "Only people who have given birth know the horror, but no one tells anyone who isn't yet a member?"

All the women nodded.

"But you did it twice," Petra said to Tabby. "If it was really that bad the first time, why would you do it again?"

"I don't think I've ever even told you how it really was," she said. "The true story. You know I had two home births. What you don't know is that during both, I ran into the kitchen to find a knife to slit my wrists. The first time, I actually had the knife in my hand before Johannes wrestled it off me. The second time, I made it to the kitchen, but the bastard had already hidden everything sharp."

Petra's mouth fell open. "But," she said, "the second time, you had a child already, so you knew it would pass, that pain. And you knew how it feels to be a mum."

"Didn't matter in the moment."

No one laughed. Instead, they looked down. The table went quiet.

You are about to watch your partner join the Secret Club. They are not ready. You are not ready either. Neither was I. How could I have been? All the daddy-to-be books I'd been gifted skipped the actual birth process entirely. As if the men starring in them had been at home, shirtless, tiny pencils behind their ears, thumbs tucked into the tops of their tool belts, staring at the piles of driftwood they were about to turn into cribs when the doorbell rang. As if when they opened it, they found their baby swaddled up on the mat. As if after scooping up the child in their big bucket hands, they saluted the stork as it flew away. As if when they shut the door, they were fathers. On the next page: "10 Ultimate Nappy-Changing Hacks!"

Reading those books, I was sure some important interim step had been left out. A grand entrance. A great expulsion. A process so traumatic that 25 percent of women experience post-traumatic stress disorder from it. Was there not something to know there? Some way I could help Evelyn not become part of that frighteningly high statistic?

Yes, there was. But no one was talking to me honestly about it either.

I'm going to let you into the Secret Club. It's time.

The Birth, Part 1: You Will Be Too Early

Every birth is unique; every birth is the same. I'll tell you about ours, and in between, I'll break into *italics* to talk about what you might expect during yours.

Our birth story begins in our favourite Vietnamese restaurant as we're waiting for our starters. I was deciding whether I should tell Evelyn about Petra and Tabby and the Secret Club when she jumped a little in her chair.

"Ooooh," she said. "That was a bad one."

It was one day before our official due date.

About 5 percent of babies are born on their due date.66 percent happen within seven days of the due date[1]. Labour induction usually happens two weeks after the due date. Your partner is slightly more likely to have a late birth than an early one if it's her first.

"Let's do this," I said, giving a single, mighty, thunderous clap. "Let's have a goddamn baby!" I waved at the server and gestured for the bill. We had no time for food. Our baby was afoot, finally.

"Hold on," she said. "If we leave this table before I get my dumplings, there's going to be a murder, never mind a birth."

"You sure we have time?"

She laughed.

I settled back into my seat. "Fine. Okay."

We finished dinner, including dessert, which I ate fast, and from the front of my chair, and didn't even really taste. During the meal, Evelyn's contractions became regular, fast, and hard. Stronger than the Braxton Hicks dress rehearsals she'd been having for... eons. Something in her body language told me she knew this was it. The big one. Splash-down. B-Day.

I looked under the table.

"What are you doing?" she asked.

"Checking to see if your water broke."

She pinched her nose. There was a bit of dumpling on her cheek, but out of spite, I didn't tell her.

"What?"

"Did you read up on birth?" she asked.

I swatted the air. "The daddy books didn't really cover it. I think because you can't, like, hack it or make a listicle about it, you know?"

As we learned back in the quiz, only 8–10 percent of people have their water break before labour begins. This is known as a "sponta-neous rupture of membranes," and it happens in 100 percent of TV births because it's dramatic and fun to shoot and, at this point, after like seventy years of TV births, no one accepts a birth without the wet-knee shot.

. . .

As I gobbled the last of my lychee ice cream, she moaned through a heavy contraction, gripping the table edge. "Wow," she said, when it was over. "That was bad. Like, seven out of ten bad."

I signalled the server to make haste with the bill. Butterflies frolicked in the meadows of my stomach. I was full to my brim with optimism. We burst back out to the street. Or rather I did and she walked really slowly, holding her lower back and groaning like an angry troll who'd just been tricked by someone crossing her bridge.

"We have time," she said, again.

I didn't know it then, but these were actually the truest words ever spoken. While Caesarean births are speedy, around two hours, max, a first-time vaginal birth takes between twelve and eighteen hours—nearly a full, miserable rotation of the Earth. Within that time, you can expect the pushing phase to be around three hours.

Birth is a marathon, not a sprint. Actually, it's more like four marathons. If you're in a restaurant, you not only have enough time to finish lunch, you probably have time to sit there until they're serving dinner. And you might still be hanging around for breakfast.

If you have so much fun the first time that you have to go again, the second birth is way shorter, usually eight hours or less.

We made it home, stopping halfway up the fourth flight of stairs so she could have a little wheezing break. In our living room, I put on a playlist I'd prepared. It was comprised of atmospheric birth songs—a suggestion from one of the books. But because I'm the booby of the universe and my naivety knows no bounds, I'd made the playlist forty-two minutes long.

"Open the app," she said. "The next one's coming."

I swiped to the contraction app and hit start.

"How you doing?" I asked, for the fifth time in ten minutes.

"Wow," she said, as she tigered around the living room then screamed for a while. "That was a bad one."

"How bad?"

"Seven out of ten."

"Well, you're doing great. Can I help you with something?"

"Yes, you can turn off this annoying music."

A minute passed. Then another. Then another. Then another. Then another. Then another. *Contraction*. The first tears.

"That was a bad one," she said. "Seven out of ten."

A minute passed. Then another. Then another. Then another. Then another. Then another. *Contraction*. More tears.

A minute passed. Then another. Then another. Then another. Then another. Then another. *Contraction*. More tears.

A minute passed. Then another. Then another. Then another. Then another. Then another. *Contraction*. More tears.

You getting the pattern? Well, it repeated a lot. Then some more. Then again.

"Can I help?" I asked, at some point. She laughed deeply, as if her suffering were *War and Peace* and my help were a haiku about yoghurt.

A minute passed. Then another. Then another. Then another. Then another. Then another. *Contraction*. Many, many tears.

The minutes were long, stretchy, as if they were wearing

elastic. I pulsed with adrenaline, but it had nowhere to go. I started to tiger around with her.

"Sit down," she said. "You're getting in my way."

"Okay. Can I help—"

She laughed deeply, as if her pain were an endless symphony and my help were a single rest note.

A minute passed. Then another. Then another. Then another. Then another. *Contraction.* Screaming. Tears. Pleading.

"Can I—"

"No," she barked. "Just leave me alone."

"Okay."

A minute passed. Then another. Then another. Then another. *Contraction.* Screaming. Sobbing. Begging. More pacing.

"Back rub?"

"Fuck off."

"Shall we do the breathing—"

She walked to the bedroom and slammed the door.

A minute passed. Then another. Then another. Then another. Then another. *Contraction.* Screaming. Tears. Pleading.

I wondered if the neighbours could hear. I laughed. Of course the neighbours could hear. Beirut could hear.

"That was a really bad one," she shouted. "Seven point five out of ten."

A minute passed. Then another. Then another. Then another. Then another. *Contraction.* Louder screaming. Louder tears. Louder pleading.

The cycle repeated for a long time, then a bit more. They estimate the universe to be about 4.54 billion years old. This evening felt longer. As if we'd arrived at the Big Bang a billion years early to get good seats.

I went and knocked on the door.

Adam Fletcher

"LEAVE ME ALONE."

"Okay, honey. You're doing great."

The door opened. "That one was an eight out of ten. Maybe it's best I'm not alone."

"Should I come in?"

"I'll come out."

"Magic."

She came out. The contractions increased in severity and frequency for another hour, until they were happening every five minutes or so. She skulked around the apartment, howling, crying, begging various gods for mercy, sometimes taking a brief break to bleed on something. I offered her everything, anything, all of it, the entire world on a string, the moon dipped in peanut butter. Unfortunately, I couldn't provide the only thing she actually wanted—labour to end. And so, she accepted nothing from me. Nothing but pushing start and stop on the app.

When the cervix begins to open, don't worry if there's clear pink or slightly bloody discharge coming from the vagina. This is the mucous plug that blocks the cervical opening during pregnancy.

This first stage of birth has two phases—early labour and active labour. In early labour, the cervix dilates and effaces. Contractions will be mostly mild and somewhat irregular. Many people confuse early for active and go to the hospital too soon.

As a benchmark, expect early labour to last for six to twelve hours and for contractions to happen anywhere from every five to every fifteen minutes, each lasting sixty to ninety seconds.

During active labour, the cervix dilates from six centimetres to ten centimetres. Contractions become stronger, closer together, and devastatingly painful. Active labour often lasts four to eight hours but can go longer. While it's not an exact science, you can expect the cervix to dilate approximately one centimetre per hour.

. . .

"Shall we go to the hospital?" I asked, somewhere around hour six.

"Yes," she said.

I ordered a cab on my phone because while what we were doing was ancient, we were doing it in a shiny, modern, flashbang world.

"First baby?" the taxi driver asked, as he pulled out of our street.

"First baby."

"Last," Evelyn snapped, as another contraction overcame her. She screamed, her hand tugging furiously on the seat belt.

"St Joseph's is a good hospital," the driver said, about our destination. "We had our kids there. Two sets of twins."

I gripped the seat. "*Two* sets of twins?"

"All boys."

"Damn." I thought about how Evelyn's boss had said everyone secretly hopes for a girl. Two contractions later, we pulled up outside the hospital. I tipped lavishly because, well, two sets of twins, all boys.

"Good luck," he said.

We were led into a small room full of bleeping, blooping diagnostic machines. "Are your contractions happening every three to five minutes?" the nurse asked, as a woman nearby screamed as if shot in both legs. The sound rattled the walls. And my eyes.

"Sometimes," Evelyn said. "Maybe more like every seven minutes?"

"Six," I corrected, because I was the App Man, dammit.

"Six," the nurse repeated, with disappointment. "Okay, let's have a look then."

Evelyn lay down and spread her legs, and we waited as

the nurse snapped on a rubber glove. The big moment. How far along were we? How much was behind us? *Five centimetres*, I chanted, silently.

The nurse felt Evelyn's cervix then sighed. "You're maybe a centimetre. Sorry."

Since women can't really check their dilation themselves, almost everyone gets the timing wrong and goes to the hospital too early. If she's fewer than five centimetres, they'll probably just send you home again. Which isn't a big deal. As with anything medical, it's always better to be too cautious than too cavalier. If she doesn't feel safe any more, go to the hospital.

Evelyn's head fell back against the bed. She wailed and sobbed. I pulled out my phone—we were seven hours in.

"I'm sorry too," I said. No one answered. No one cared what I was. Another enormous, bloodcurdling scream ripped through the wall. I covered my ears.

"You can stay here if you want," the nurse said, looking towards the sound. "But it's a hospital, you know?"

We knew.

"I'm sorry," Evelyn said, getting up.

"It's fine," the nurse said reassuringly. "Everyone comes too early the first time. *Everyone*. You've a long way to go yet. Go home and relax as much as possible. At some point, you won't feel safe there any more and you'll know it's time to come back."

"Okay," Evelyn said.

"Okay," I said, and ordered another taxi.

We waited outside for not more than a minute. A taxi pulled up. Same driver. "Everyone goes too early," he lamented. "Well, not my wife…"

"Two sets of twins," I said, shaking my head. He sucked in a slow breath. "All boys."

Evelyn sat there. Crushed. Shocked. Looking at her face, I thought of Hiroo Onoda, a Japanese soldier who fought in World War II. He was deployed to the Philippines to conduct guerrilla warfare, and because of communication break-downs, he never received the official notification that the war had ended, in 1945.

So, he kept on fighting.

They dropped pamphlets.

He got them but assumed they were enemy propaganda.

So, he kept on fighting.

They dropped more pamphlets. He got them but assumed they were enemy propaganda, too.

So, he kept on fighting.

They rigged up loudspeakers and blasted messages at him. He heard them but assumed they were enemy propaganda.

So, he kept on fighting. He said he'd stop only if they flew out his former commander, who, by now, was a bookseller.

They flew the bookseller out.

Hiroo did finally surrender. In 1974[2]. It must have been a really embarrassing press conference. Evelyn's face was how I imagined Hiroo's must have looked during that press conference. It said, *I fought a thirty-year war, alone. And I lost.*

The taxi driver parked outside our apartment building. What was I supposed to tip this time? That was a hell of a tip, that first tip. I'd really gone into the cookie jar for this father of twin twins. I couldn't tip like that again because assuming our child would be born in the next billion years—something I was doubting—she'd need clothes and food and might one day want to go to university, or Mars.

I didn't tip.

Not a cent.

The Birth, Part 2: Endure, Just Endure

Back at home, we were sadness personified. Not only were we failing at birth, we were failing slowly: the worst way to fail.

I put the birth playlist back on, but Evelyn howled through its most banging tunes. To my surprise, she didn't appreciate the inclusion of "I'm Coming Out," by Diana Ross, or "Push It," by Salt-N-Pepa.

I turned it off.

The mood was sombre. I sniffed and smelt eternity.

"We need to call Marina," Evelyn said, around hour ten, I think, because time was wobbling like jelly in a hurricane. The contractions she'd been enduring recently were of a different calibre.

"But it's the middle of the night," I protested.

"Something is wrong."

"What do you mean something is wrong?"

"Something is really wrong."

I called the midwife.

"Is it supposed to feel like this?" Evelyn asked.

"Describe a contraction," Marina asked, her voice thick with sleep.

"It feels as if I'm being burned alive and then the flames are put out by acid."

There was a pause, and I recognised in it a person scrabbling together words they hoped would be diplomatic. "That sounds like a contraction," Marina said. "This is birth. I'm sorry."

"Oh," Evelyn said, becoming still. In her face, I saw more shock than pain.

"Balls," she said.

"How close together are they?" Marina asked.

I looked down at the app. "Every four minutes."

"Don't go to the hospital," Marina said. We looked at each other and then at the floor. The silence was heavy with deceit. "Have you already been?"

"Thanks," I said, and hung up.

A minute passed. Then another. Then another. Then another. *Contraction.* SCREAM. "Oh god. Oh god. Shit. Fuck. I can't. I can't do this."

"You can do this. You're doing great."

"I'm not. I suck at this. I can't do it any more. I can't. There's no way. Oh god. I can't do this. My legs. Fuck."

I handed her some tissues. She handed them back.

A minute passed. Then another. Then another. Then another. *Contraction.* SCREAM. "Oh god. Oh god. Shit. Fuck. I can't. I can't do this."

"Seven out of ten?" I asked.

"A thousand out of ten."

"You can do this. You're doing great."

"I'm not. I'm not. I'm not." She stomped around the living room. "There's just no way. Oh god. I can't do this. My legs. *Fuck.*"

"Can I do something?"

She laughed deeply, as if her suffering were a great void and I had arrived at it armed with only a howl.

Mostly, she was the one doing the howling. I went to the kitchen to make some toast for myself. While I was spreading peanut butter across its crisp, hot surface, Evelyn let out a scream like the woman in the hospital, as if a demon were splitting her in two, for fun, with a spoon. I put the knife down, licked my finger, and pushed start on the contraction app. I picked up a slice of toast and then, while the person I loved most in the world shouted, for the first time, that she wanted to die, I bit down on its crust. After she said, again, that no, really, she wanted to die, I hid all the knives behind the cookbooks.

I found her hyperventilating in the corner of what was ready to be our daughter's room. I sat on the edge of the bed with my toast, feeling as useless as an oven glove at an orgy.

"Stop it," she said, as I chewed.

"But I'm not doing anything?" I said, and then realised she meant the app. I stopped the app.

She was slumped on the floor, crying, her back to the wall. I was crying rather a lot now too, into my toast. I went to hug her. She pushed me away. I got up and found a fresh towel to clean the blood off her legs while thinking that this was the worst day of my life, but it wasn't, not really, because it wasn't a time of my life. I'd disassociated. I was merely a contraction-app-starting-mildly-weeping-peanut-butter-toast-eating apparition.

"Oh god," Evelyn said. "It's coming again." She flapped her hands in front of her face. "Oh no. Oh god. I can't do this. I can't do this."

I pushed start on the app. Another contraction shattered her, and to avoid watching it, I closed my eyes and thought about all the many years of our lives where we hadn't known each other. Thirty-three of them we had lived innocently, unaware that our trajectories would smash into each other, causing this awful moment. I thought about when I first saw her, standing outside a bar just ten minutes from where we now lived, and how I said, like actually said with my mouth, "That girl is a ten."

It just came out.

But she was.

Is.

Three years and change later, we had both made her want to die. I had to conclude we'd gone astray. Couldn't we have just got a labradoodle? At some point, her wailing subsided, and I pushed stop on the app. We were down to three minutes now, sometimes less.

"I can't do it," she said, and for the first time, I wondered if she might be right. I didn't say that, of course. I didn't say anything, even though there were a million empty motivational messages I could have offered:

You can do it.

You're doing great.

Billions of women have already done it.

You can do it.

You're doing great.

Nearly there.

Think of the baby.

Think about how good it will feel to hold your baby.

You can do this.

But she was smart, my woman, and would recognise immediately that these weren't the authentic contents of the soul neither of us believed I had. They would annoy her more than my silence.

So, I said very little at all. "Back massage?" I tried, at one point, and she laughed as if her suffering were a galaxy and my help were a single grain of sand on a single stretch of beach on a single distant planet in a single star system so mediocre no one had even bothered to map it.

Another contraction. There should be more words for *contraction*.

I helped her up, and she spread her feet, tipped back her head, opened her mouth, and bellowed, hands on the wall. I sobbed into a tissue. I took away the towel and gave her some water.

We endured. Time passed, I suppose, just about, possibly.

She paced. I paced too. I said, occasionally, that I was sorry this was happening to her and that if I could take it from her, or assuage it, I would. And that was the truth.

Well, maybe not the whole truth. I wouldn't have taken, like, *all* of it. I might have borrowed it for a few minutes, the pain, just to check it out, like a library book. Then I'd have given it back and run away somewhere. I was finding the idea of running away very seductive. I wondered if it was too late to abscond to Darkest Peru? The reverse Paddington Bear.

"That was a long one," she said, an indeterminate number of contractions later. C-bombs?

"Yes," I said. "One minute forty-seven."

I looked round the room at all the things we'd cried into and all the things she'd bled on, knocked over, thrown, kicked, splashed with her bodily fluids. All the things I'd sprinkled with toast crumbs. It was a crime scene, and she was its victim. I was, at best, a rubbernecker slowing down to watch.

"Hospital," she said.

I ordered a taxi, silently praying it wouldn't be the same driver.

The Birth, Part 3: Smell Your Children

"ARGGGGHHGHGHGHGHGHGHHDOHGODKILLMEO-HICANTARGHGHGHHGHGHGHGHGFUUCUCUCU-CUCCCKKKKKKKKKKKKKKKKSHITTTT!" Evelyn said, as I helped her into the backseat of the night's third taxi. "I can't do this."

"You've already done most of it."

"I can't."

"You are."

"Masks?" I asked, because pandemic.

"No need," the driver said. I strapped myself in. "First kid?" His eyebrows were thick rugs that touched each other. The middle of the night was flirting hard with the early morning. Between Evelyn and me was the go bag, or, since it had already been, the going again bag.

"Yes," I said, then looked away, because we were many, many hours (twelve? fifteen? four hundred and seven?) into our misery and my nerves were quivering. I either wanted to watch my child (finally) be born, or, like Evelyn, I just wanted to die. The first was my preference, but honestly, the preference was slight. And if this was how I felt, how must she be feeling?

I didn't know how she was feeling. I asked sometimes, but language has its limits and she'd reached them.

"Smell your children," the taxi driver said, as he pulled out. "They smell fantastic."

"Yes," I said, wearily, without looking up.

"Really, take the time to smell your children. Men are always about work, you know? But they grew up so fast, the children. I have two. They were born here."

I assumed he meant in Berlin and not in his taxi, although if he drove any slower…

I looked up and saw him tilting the rearview mirror towards me. "I did everything for her," he said, each sentence snapping shut. "The mother. She left me. I see them. The kids. When I can."

"Did you stay home with them?" I asked.

He blew a raspberry. "Men can't stay home with the kids. That's for the women. Women are patient. We're not patient."

I was going to stay home. It was agreed. I was looking forward to it.

"ARGGGGHHGHGHHHGHGHGHGHGHHGHGHGH-HGHGUFUUCUCUCUCUCCCK-KKKKKKKKKKKKKKKKSHITTTT!"

"Oooh," the taxi driver said, when Evelyn had finished screaming. "That was a bad one. Women are better than men," he continued. "They need to stay home. We make the money, pay for the family." He glanced at Evelyn in the mirror. "Try not to get blood on the seats if you can."

I gripped the seat tighter. I would prove this stupid, hick, throwback taxi man wrong. I wasn't going to be a father to my child but a second mother. This man lazily revered mothers but didn't respect them. If he respected them, he wouldn't dump the work he didn't want to do on them, wrapping their burden as privilege. I mean, the audacity. No, idiot, everything Evelyn was going to do, I would do too. Our child would know only parental abundance. Mama, Papa—it would be the same to her. I didn't know how because I didn't have breasts with which to feed her, but I would find a way. There were probably fake ones on Amazon that squirted milk like tiny nipple water pistols.

I turned my head to Evelyn. Her back was arched. Her eyes were tightly closed. She was far from here, and far from good.

"I did everything for my kids," he said. *Except stay home, yeah.* "And yet, she still left."

"Hmm," I said, staring out the window as we passed several giant overflowing black bins and smashed glass bottles littering uneven pavements. A bus stop that had become a homeless shelter. A drunk man who wobbled out of a bar, fell down a step, and toppled over. He kept singing. Why did we live in this prison? It wasn't good enough for my child. We'd leave for Narnia first thing tomorrow, through the wardrobe.

"I bought everything for them," the man droned on. "For Christmas. New crib. New bicycle. Everything new. Still, she left me."

We had nothing new. It was all passed down through the baby chain. The Sisterhood. This man could learn a lot from the Sisterhood, as I was.

"Again," Evelyn said, taking deep breaths. I pressed start on the app. "ARGGHHGHHGHGODKILLMEOHICAN-TARGHGHGHHGHGHGHGHGUFUUCUCUCUCUCC-CKKKKKKKKKSHITTTT!"

"No job is more special than mother," he said. "Staying at home all day with them? That isn't for men. We would go crazy. No patience. They like it, even."

Evelyn's head snapped forwards. "I don't have any more

fucking patience. Okay? Just drive faster and stop saying all this nonsense."

It was quiet for a minute. The driver angled the mirror away from her and towards me, bouncing his eyebrows as he did so. *She's a handful*, the look said, continuing his unbroken record of extreme wrongness. Because she wasn't.

Isn't.

She didn't need to be handled. She deftly handled. Required little, as evidenced by both her pregnancy and, now, labour, where once again, there was nothing I could do for her. She was powerful and self-sufficient and smarter than him and me combined. Wiser too.

It was imperative our daughter see this magnificent woman out in the world, using her gifts to make it better, so she would know she could, too. So she would know that a woman's place is anywhere she wants it to be.

We pulled up to the hospital. He turned off the engine. I didn't tip.

"Smell your children," he said, as we got out.

The Birth, Part 4: Some Women Like It When...

We were led into the same diagnostic room as before. Nearby, a different woman (I hoped) emitted a primal scream.

The nurse we'd seen last time came in. How had her shift not ended yet? It felt as if our last visit had been a month ago. We'd been different people then. Not so chewed up. Spat out. Picked back up again. Chewed some more. Spat back out.

"Hello again," she said. "How regular are you now, then?"

"Every minute or two," I said, proudly. As if I'd done the work to make that happen.

"Let's have a look-see." I helped Evelyn onto the bed and the nurse snapped on the glove and gave her a good prodding.

"Seven centimetres," the nurse said excitedly. "That's fantastic. That's brilliant. We need to get you to a birthing room right away."

"Yes," Evelyn shouted, and I grabbed her and we sobbed into each other's shoulders. It was a tender moment—the first in hours. "We're nearly there," she said. "It's nearly over."

"Yes, my love."

We were led into a birthing room that combined the glum austerity of a hospital with the facilities of a midrange hotel. There was a bed but also a kidney-shaped bath, some kind of bondage-looking birthing chair, and a yoga ball. We then met our hospital midwife, who was small and smiley and young enough to be our daughter. "Seven centimetres, I hear? Respect." Her hands were shaking. "I'm new," she said, quietly. Everything she did, she did quietly.

"How new?" I asked.

"First week."

"That's okay," Evelyn said, still high on the fact that she was so far along and that she'd endured so much alone. Well, with me, but that was the same thing.

Hell opened its gates and released another contraction that rendered Evelyn demonic. Her body clamped and her face twisted and she halved in size. Death was there too; I glimpsed its bony face. After spending another thousand hours with her in the fiery pits, the contraction ascended, freeing her, briefly. I was no longer tracking them. They came too often. Evelyn prowled this new room as she had the ones before, enduring a few more C-bombs, then said she needed the toilet. I helped her in there, pulling the IV pole behind her. Then I went to the window to resume my favoured companionship activity: scratching my head and looking pensive.

The midwife approached me and lowered her already low voice to that of a conspiratorial whisper. "Some women," she said, "like it when you massage their back."

I stared.

I blinked.

I laughed.

"Sorry," I said. "I didn't mean to laugh."

She slunk back to her station, where she pretended to mark things on a sheet of paper. Evelyn returned, chased out of the toilet by another contraction, then another, then another, then more, then all of them. Then she was back in the toilet. The midwife approached again as we heard Evelyn puking. "Some women—"

"Look," I snapped, now knowing how I must have made Evelyn feel over the past hours with my inane suggestions. "I know you mean well, but we're fourteen hours in. Anything you can think to offer I've already offered a dozen times."

"Okay," the midwife said, slinking back to her station, where she pretended to mark things on a sheet of paper. I remembered how Robbie Williams had said that watching your partner give birth is like watching your favourite pub burn down. He'd said nothing about how long it took to burn, though.

Evelyn emerged from the bathroom. "What are my options for pain?"

"You could try a Buscopan," the midwife said.

"It's useless."

"Laughing gas?"

"Okay. Do it."

The midwife hooked up the laughing gas. When the next contraction seized her, Evelyn sucked madly on the gas for a few breaths then pulled off the mask and launched it at the wall. "What else?" she demanded. "I need more."

"An epidural?" said the midwife. "But it can slow down birth."

"I don't care if the birth lasts a thousand years, just as long as it doesn't feel like this any more."

"I've already sent the anaesthesiologist home."

"Why did you do that?" Evelyn asked, as if the midwife had just peed all over her face.

"You're doing so well," the midwife said, but then looked up at the clock. "*Were* doing so well."

"Call him back. NOW."

139

The midwife ran for the phone.

Epidurals are used in 60 percent of births in the US, 30 percent in the UK, and 25 percent in Germany, yet there's still some snootiness around them, as if the women who opt for them are cheating, somehow. There's nothing natural about pain. When in pain, the only thing natural is to try to minimise it. Epidurals minimise pain. Some studies have found they can slow down birth, but the evidence isn't overwhelming, and for many women, the duration is less important than the intensity of their suffering.

An epidural involves injecting anaesthesia near the bottom of the spine, to block nerve impulses in the lower back. The goal is diminished pain, not total numbness, so she's still alert, can feel the contractions and push. If she knows that she wants one, it's best to ask early, which we obviously didn't do.

Because birth can be so frenetic, some couples create a birth plan, which they give to their care providers (birth plans are not customary in Germany). The plan might stipulate, among other things, which pain-relief methods they want, whether forceps or vacuum extraction can be used, whether to delay cord clamping (cutting the umbilical cord), and how soon after birth they want skin-to-skin contact with the baby. Even if you create a birth plan together, she's the one in existential levels of pain, so if she decides she's suddenly pro-epidural (Evelyn hadn't planned to use one), she can change the plan. You can't.

My stomach growled. Having had no idea it would take this long, we'd eaten all the food in the bag except for a pack of wasabi nuts, which Evelyn must have packed, because I really, really hate wasabi.

The anaesthesiologist arrived looking frazzled. "I was halfway home."

He gave her the epidural, and finally, I watched Evelyn relax. There was still pain, but it was hour-four pain, not hour fourteen. She smiled through the next contraction, such was the relief.

"Did I just crap myself?" she asked, several contractions later.

"Yes, hunny."

"I've been worried about doing that."

"It's the second time."

"Oh."

"Don't worry about it."

"Fan me," she said, and my relief was exquisite, for this was something I could do. I COULD BE THE FAN MAN, I COULD.

The midwife gave me a handheld fan. I fanned like no one had ever fanned before. I fanned like I was her biggest fan, and also a fan of fans, and fanning.

I fanned, basically.

And then fanned harder.

An entire blissful, purposeful minute later, Evelyn grabbed the fan and threw it on the floor. "You're fanning wrong," she said. I lowered my head; the shame tasted worse than wasabi nuts. Almost.

"It's taking too long," the midwife said. "The baby is growing stressed. If it takes too much longer, we're going to have to consider a Caesarean."

About 21 percent of births happen via C-sections[1]. Like many women who have epidurals, many women who have C-sections suffer from the idea that they've cheated, even though Caesarean births come with more blood loss and an increased risk of infection, take longer to recover from, and result in longer hospital stays than vaginal births. There are also some minor immune system disad-

vantages for the baby, since they're not exposed to as much helpful bacteria as they would be during a vaginal exit. It's fast, but it's no cheat. There is no cheat. I think there would be by now, if men had to give birth. Apple would have invented some kind of external iWomb. Uber would deliver the baby to us at home, wrapped up like a burrito. Aged five.

We got a new midwife. This one was older, wiser, sterner. She said the baby had gone backwards, as if she had looked at this world in all its draped finery, wrinkled her tiny, booger-congested nose, and said, "Nah, that's not for me."

"Your baby needs to come out now," the new midwife said. "It was going well, but it's not any more. Sorry. I need more from you. I need you to push."

"I don't know how to push," said Evelyn.

"You do."

"Obviously I don't."

"We'll do it together." The nurse leapt onto the bed and clamped down on Evelyn's stomach. "Grab a leg," she said to me.

"Which leg?"

"Any."

I took a leg and pushed down on it and another nurse was called in and grabbed the other leg and as the next contraction descended we all screamed "PUSH!" at Evelyn but she protested that she was already pushing and then the new midwife said "Pretend you're doing a shit" and that clicked something and Evelyn pushed from a lower place and they said the baby was moving again and this realisation buoyed everyone, especially Evelyn, and we did some more shouting and clamping and now a different nurse or midwife or interested passing stranger was tugging on the baby's head, which crowned, finally.

Wait… I could see the baby's head?!

That meant I'd soon be able to see the whole baby, didn't it? Which meant it must be nearly over. I was so shocked I dropped Evelyn's leg.

"It's coming!" I shouted. "I can see it!" It was all one big contraction now.

"Yes, yes, yes, yes!" the new midwife shouted. "More. I NEED MORE." She was all-up in Evelyn's face. "You don't stop. You don't stop. *More.* I need more from you. It's nearly over. YOU'RE ABOUT TO MEET YOUR BABY," she shouted, and, with brilliant comic timing, our daughter, Runa, popped out, followed shortly by about an octopus's worth of afterbirth and placenta.

Not bad, I thought. Not bad at all, those "I NEED MORE" and "YOU'RE ABOUT TO MEET YOUR BABY" lines.

Evelyn let out a new scream, but its tone was softer. It was relief. "It's over?"

The nurse rushed off with the baby and I fell down onto Evelyn and we slobbered all over each other and she asked again and again if it was really over and if Runa was really okay and I told her yes, it was really over, and yes, Runa was really okay, and we kissed and I was awed by what she had endured for us. I'd never felt love for anyone, even her, like the love I felt in that moment. It wasn't even close.

She was, without doubt, my Hiroo.

She had joined the Secret Club. I had seen its initiation ceremony up close. I silently vowed to never do so again.

"Cut the cord," the midwife said, several minutes later. And then, for the first time, I saw my daughter properly. She was a giant bruised wrinkle. Hairy too. Apparently, what they say about heartburn is true. There was actually a bit of the labradoodle about her. She looked as exhausted as her mother. She squawked once, but without conviction. I cut the cord. It was rubbery. The nurse took her away again and cleaned her up some more. It was all very professional and methodical, as if we'd picked a fish from a tank in a fancy seafood restaurant and they were preparing to cook it.

"Someone would like to meet you," the midwife said, finally, when she'd cleaned Runa and made her look fractionally less like an alien raisin. She handed her, swaddled, to Evelyn, who accepted her to her chest.

"Hi," she said, folding inwards and letting out a low, primal, mammalian moan. It was unlike any sound I'd ever heard her make. And I'd heard a lot of them the past, endless, day and night. It was the moan of a lion nuzzling at a new cub. It was the moan of an orca reunited with a lost calf. It was the moan of a baby elephant as it sits with its mother who has been shot in the face by poachers who want to grind her tusks into soup that idiots think will give them stronger erections.

It was neither happy nor sad, this moan. It was simply a bellowing of ancient reverence; the soundtrack of someone's private universe being rearranged. She was imprinting on our child. I wouldn't have believed it if I hadn't witnessed it. Doing so, I considered the possibility, fleetingly, that everything was going to be just peachy.

"It's you," she said to Runa, sweetly. "I know you. There you are. *Hi*. This is your…" She looked over at me. "What are you doing?"

"Nothing," I said, discreetly slipping the last wasabi nut into my mouth. I chewed and swallowed. "Oooh, that was a bad one. Seven out of ten."

The Birth, Part 5: Family

We were on the maternity ward in a family room, praise COVID. Runa was awake. She and I were cuddling, skin-to-skin. She was about the size of my hand, and I held her against my chest. Her face was deliciously wonky. Her eyes had my shape and Evelyn's colour. The cuddle was as close to perfection as I'd ever experienced. Long-limbed angels harped, and I melted in the blazing heat of all my blessings. Evelyn was dozing next to us in the bed. We were more than the sum of our parts; we were a family.

The birth had taken so long that Runa had ingested her own waste, and because of that and fears of jaundice, we'd have to stay in the hospital for a few days. Nurses came in, nurses went out; we couldn't control it. I didn't mind. They relaxed me. They were caring for our child, and by watching them, I was learning how to care for her. And Evelyn was getting the time she needed to sleep and recover.

Evelyn's eyes fluttered open.

"Hey," I said. "How you doing?"

"Good. Did they say anything new?"

"Other than that she looks a bit like a character in *The Simpsons*, she's perfect."

"And the wonkiness?"

"Minor, and she'll grow out of it. How are you feeling?"

"I keep having nightmares. Flashbacks."

"I know. You're screaming in your sleep."

"Really?"

I lifted her hand and kissed it. "It's over. Runa's here now. It was all for something."

She took a deep breath. "I feel like I just spent time in a torture prison and, when I was on my way out, they presented me with a stuffed unicorn. And now everyone keeps saying, 'Look at your lovely unicorn. You must be so happy with your unicorn.' And all I can think is, 'I don't care about the unicorn—I care about what just happened to me. I care about the torture.' Does that make me a bad mother?"

"No, of course not."

"Why was any of that necessary?"

I teared up. "I don't know, and you're right. You're completely right."

"But it's not her fault," she said, looking down at Runa. "Poor little thing."

"What do you feel when you look at her?" I asked, worried that the experience of birthing Runa had tainted Runa.

"Overwhelming love," she said, without hesitation.

I wept. "I'm sorry," I said, looking down, trying to suppress my sobs. "It will get better."

"How will it get better?"

"The memory of it will fade."

She laughed. "Trust me. It won't."

It did, of course. Birth, something she talked about every day at first, became something she talked about every other day, then once a week, then once a month. Now, she talks about it only if she meets a woman who has just joined the Secret Club and wants to compare notes/outrage.

For the month after the birth, every time Evelyn told her birth story, I'd burst into tears, excuse myself, and leave. I was so shocked by the strength of the reaction that I did some research, and I learned that, actually, many men are traumatised by watching their partner give birth. It's poorly researched, as the research around the woman's trauma is more pressing. In fact, you might find the idea of the partner having a lingering adverse reaction ridiculous, but… is it?

For twenty hours—that felt like a hundred million hours —I was useless (or so it felt) while the person I loved most in the world was split apart by the person I would probably, at some point, love most in the world. And I just had to endure that. Could do nothing to make it better or, instead of that, just make it end already.

Evelyn encouraged me to talk to my male friends, many of whom had recently had children, to see if they were having a hard time processing the experience. I brought it up on the next boys' night, maybe a month after the birth. I told them how I kept spontaneously crying and how I often had nightmares. I used the T-word. It got a lot of sniggers.

"Traumatised?" my friend James said. "Seriously?"

"Yeah, your vagina still sore?" mocked another.

"I didn't even know you were pregnant," quipped a third, Mark. "You hid it well under that beer gut."

"Oh, come on," I said. "None of you found it really hard watching your partner going through that?"

"Nah," said Mark. "It was fine, really. It just went on sooooo long."

"Yeah," said James. "I just sat around like a useless sack of shit. I can see now why they used to leave the men outside smoking cigars in the waiting room."

"You'd have rather been outside?"

He considered it. "If there'd been a TV. I mean, I was helping her do the breathing exercises and stuff, but that got really repetitive."

"She wanted those?" I asked.

"Yeah." He frowned. "I mean, I think so?"

"Did any of you cry during it?"

"Why would I cry?"

"I saw you cry two weeks ago when Arsenal lost."

"That's different," he said, leaning back. "That was against Tottenham."

I've since talked to many fathers about their birth experience. While the specifics vary, we all seem to have one thing in common: we felt as if we were useless. But feelings—as pervasive as they are—are not reality.

"I felt much less alone because you were there," Evelyn said, in the days following the birth. "I don't know if I expressed it, but I felt it, throughout. And you probably didn't notice you were doing it, but you ran interference for me with the midwives and doctors, making sure nothing happened that I didn't want to happen. I'm not going to pretend I couldn't have done it without you, but I'm glad I didn't have to."

There is much you offer, even if she says no to everything you offer. You can still support, mop up, fan, cheer, remind to breathe, give back rubs, massage temples, ask questions, and run interference. In the downtime, and there will be A LOT of downtime, you have a voice, so use it. Tell her how sorry you are that this is happening to her. Tell her how proud of her you are. Tell her she isn't alone. Tell her you love her. Tell her this will end. Tell her how excited you are to meet your child. Tell her how you felt when you two first met. Tell her how you first knew that you loved her. Tell her what you love most about her. Tell her how you feel about her right now. Tell her you hope the kid gets her nose. Tell her you can't believe she packed those goddamn wasabi nuts.

It's not much, but it's not nothing either.

Love Is an Act

During the birth, your partner is flooded with the bonding hormone oxytocin (it's what triggers the birth to begin). By the time the whole ordeal is over and she has the swaddled baby in her arms, she's so primed to love, she'll likely dissolve into a sticky puddle of maternal affection, as Evelyn did. I think they could have put a Barbie in her arms and she'd have bonded deeply with it and we'd still be singing it nursery rhymes today.

It doesn't happen this seamlessly for every mother, of course, but biology does its best, and biology is really, really good; it's had a lot of time to practise.

Births don't douse dads with the same levels of oxytocin, so it's logical that the bonding process can take a little longer for us. What I felt for Runa was overshadowed by the gratitude I felt for Evelyn, whom I now saw as an Amazonian goddess.

Runa's existence was very welcome, don't get me wrong, but Evelyn's *continued* existence was far more miraculous to me. I guess if you spend enough hours hearing someone make noises that suggest they're dying, at some point it's rude not to believe them.

But she hadn't died.

And that was really, really lovely.

Also, Runa was a funny-looking little bugger and she cried vociferously whenever she did anything at all.

But I wasn't worried about what I didn't feel, partly because, through pregnancy, I'd got used to being under-whelmed, and to the Divide. Also, an anecdote from a friend of Evelyn's was looping in my head.

Two years after a traumatic birth experience, this friend was seeing a therapist while considering whether to have a second child. It had taken her six months to bond with her son, something she'd kept from her partner because she was so ashamed of it.

"I didn't love him," she said to the therapist. "I would look at him and think, 'I feel nothing.' And the guilt of that, of not loving my child, just destroyed me."

The therapist considered this, as therapist are prone to do. "What makes you think you didn't love him?"

"I know how love feels."

"Did you feed him?"

"Yes."

"Change him?"

"Yes."

"Sing, play, rock, walk, feed, hug? Sing, play, rock, walk, feed, hug?"

"Of course."

"Then you loved him. Love is an act, not a feeling. You did everything your child needed. Therefore, you loved him."

Even if what you feel for your baby is less than what you expected, your duty is only to act lovingly and trust that the rest will follow.

I trusted. "I can't believe it's true," Evelyn said to me, a few hours after the birth. She hadn't stopped looking at Runa. "So much of the stuff they tell you about pregnancy is bull-shit—I felt certain that I wouldn't feel love immediately, but I'm just besotted."

"Yes," I said, wiping away a tear. "It's lovely."

"It's not like that for you?"

"It's…" I hesitated. "Plenty. For now."

Tell Your Family and Friends

The "rule" is that you don't tell anyone when labour begins so that there's no outside clamouring for information that might distract or pressure your partner in the birthing room. No rush. No expectations.

After the birth, you might not feel like telling people right away, either. We waited a full day to tell our family Runa had been born. They've never forgiven us for this, nor has any explanation for the delay ever satisfied them. In their eyes, we are simply monsters.

I'll try to explain it again anyway, in case, after the birth, you feel like we did—that you need a little time alone.

Even with the post-birth tiredness, trauma, confusion, and disbelief, there's a special halo that surrounds brand-new parents, finally united with their child and awash with relief that mother and child made it through safely.

You both know that outside the hospital walls are myriad pesky obligations, appointments, tasks, routines, and burdens. And then there are all your life's VIPs desperate to meet the new addition and drink from your rich emotional soup. You love them, and they love you, but they all come with their own anxieties, fears, irrationalities, baggage, opinions, annoying platitudes, and unquenchable desire for updates, facts, gossip, lowdowns, and gory details.

It's a lot.

And you've already been through plenty.

Also, telling them requires you to start putting all this into words. Yet, you know that no matter how eloquently you might whisper those bent sounds down a phone line or type those bent shapes into a messaging app, they could never represent the grand, sweeping totality of what you have just witnessed—the primal, violent wonder of watching a human life enter this world. And it feels offensive to even try.

So, you don't.

Instead, you sit together in the awe for a while. That's okay. Take your time (but maybe not a whole day).

Why Didn't Anyone Warn Us?

"I'm just so exhausted," I said, as Evelyn and I lay next to each other on the hospital bed. It was two days after the birth. "I can't do this any more."

"Me neither," she said. "I've gone cross-eyed."

"It's the lack of sleep, you know?"

"Totally. And of peace. I just need five minutes to myself to think."

I nodded. "I didn't know it would be like this."

She lowered her eyes. "Me neither."

"Why didn't anyone warn us?"

"Maybe they did?" she asked. "Can we do something?"

"Shifts, maybe?" I suggested. "Working both phones."

"Your German isn't good enough."

"Hmm," I said. "Emojis then? I'm getting a lot of action out of the one with the chicken hatching from the egg followed by a thumbs up. But it's not enough for them—they want to know about times, dates, weights, middle names, how you are, how it all feels, just the nitty-goddamn-gritty of it all across forty-seven different simultaneous chats."

She frowned. "I find that emoji offensive. It didn't hatch from an egg—it ripped its way out of my body."

"Oh, right. *Yeah.*"

"I hate it when they ask what we need," she said.

"Lasagne. I always say lasagne. We got some more flowers while you were sleeping. I left them out at the nurses' station. I don't want something else to care for, especially because they're going to die on us. Who sends flowers? Who needs flowers?"

"Who sends so many messages?" she asked.

I rubbed my eyes. "They know they need to ask questions. That it shows they're a good friend. That they're interested. They just don't know that everyone we've ever met in the past five years is doing exactly the same thing, and all at once. That we're running an endless WhatsApp marathon over here."

"Did we do this too when our friends had kids?"

"Oh god," I said. "I sent flowers to Mark and Linda. Oh no, I called them too. Well, I won't do that again. Any friends go into labour, I'm going to say nothing for a week. Then I'll send them the chick hatching from the egg and a question mark. They can reply with a thumbs up. And that'll be the last they'll hear from me for a full calendar year. They can spend that time getting their shit together and waiting for their kid to become a bit interesting. Then I'll send them a beer and a question mark, and our glorious friendship can resume."

"I'll make a group," She said. "Everyone in one place. It's our best hope."

"Perfect. Good idea." I looked over at Runa, who was paused. "Is she okay? Shouldn't she, I don't know, do something?"

Evelyn wafted her hand. "Baby's fine. Just lies there like a lemon. It's everyone else who's the problem."

It's Time to Go Home

At some point, they, those kind doctors and nurses, those uniformed medical heroes, will say, "Go home." And that'll be that. Might even be the day of the birth, if all has gone well (getting to go home the same day happens less often in the US than in Europe).

Suddenly, you're about to exit the hospital doors holding a tiny person, barely larger than a bag of sugar, in a carrier.

All yours.

That's it. You're the custodian of an entire human life, and yet there's been no test. No exam. No licence. As the doors part, you feel wholly inadequate and unprepared. You smile meekly at your partner, who grins back nervously.

You step out of the hospital, out of your cocoon, and are assaulted by light and sound and colour. Has the world always been so full of people and flowers and bumblebees and whizzing scooters and growling dogs and honking cars? Has it always been so loud and so full and so teeming with IMMENSE DANGER?

You want to turn around and go back inside, to demand your hospital room back, to stay there until your child is eighteen. Instead, cautiously, you walk towards the taxi rank, or rather, you walk while your partner waddles like a duck with a fresh ponding injury.

"Ahhhh," says a woman, who stops to coo. "I remember when mine were that size. Enjoy it, won't you? It goes so fast."

"Thanks," you both say. "We will."

Enjoyment? How long after fear comes enjoyment?

"Did you see that baby?" a child says as they walk by, holding their father's hand.

"Yes," the father says. "You were like that once."

"I wasn't."

An orderly points and his colleague turns, sees you, apologises, and angles so his cigarette smoke blows in the opposite direction. You keep walking and a woman practically leaps off the pavement into the road to make way, ushering you past. A taxi draws to a slow, careful stop just ahead, like a chariot called by destiny.

"She's gorgeous," the taxi driver says, getting out to open the door.

You wonder if the world will always be this kind to you three. You wrestle with the car seat, silently cursing that stupid fatherhood book that had no practical, applicable advice and was just about mushy feelings.

You're having a lot of mushy feelings; you welcome them all without judgement. You know it's not what you feel but how you feel about what you feel.

You feel good about feelings. You're feeling new things, too, as yet undefined. You're revelling in their grandeur. The scale has blown out. It's as if you've undergone an emotion baptism.

"Let me," the driver says, nudging you aside. "I've had three."

"Wow," you say.

He has the seat installed in seconds. You climb in. The baby is between you and your partner. It gurgles. Your heartbeat, already fluttering, accelerates. As does the taxi, pulling out into traffic.

You bend down to the car seat and inhale. The aroma of your child is very pleasant. There is something sacred, maybe even ancient about that cheesy manna.

Bugger me, you think. We did it. We're parents.

You reach down and take your baby's minuscule hand, wrapping it around just one of your calloused, chipolata fingers. "We're going home," you say. "You have your own room and everything. But, I mean, you can also stay with us at first, if you want? *Cool*. Yeah, we have so much to show you. It's going to be so great, just wait and see. We're so, so happy you're here."

* * *

(Not) The End

Writing this book has been a very emotional, cathartic experience. Thank you for reading it. If you enjoyed it please leave a review/rating, it really does help.

Want to know what happened next? It wasn't what I expected. Join me for a tour through the first year of fatherhood in **Dad Differently: Babies** - the second book in the series.

It's out now. I hope to see you there.

Adam

Also by Adam Fletcher

- Non-fiction -

Dad Differently: Babies (Dad Differently Series #2)

Don't Go There (Weird Travel Series #1)

Don't Come Back (Weird Travel Series #2 and Writer's Digest
Memoir of the Year Winner)

Tuk-tuk for Two (Weird Travel Series #3)

After Happy Ever After (Weird Travel Series #4)

Lost But Not Least (an exclusive free book for my newsletter
subscribers)

That Time I Lost My Mind

Understanding the British

Fast Philosophy

- Fiction (as Adam R. Fletcher) -

The Death of James Jones, sort of

Notes

5. A Process, Not an Event

1. Machin, A (2018). *The Life of Dad: The Making of the Modern Father*. Simon & Schuster
2. Ibid
3. Ibid.

10. SuperSmeller

1. Doty RL, Cameron EL. (2009) *Sex differences and reproductive hormone influences on human odor perception.* Physiol Behav. 2009 May 25;97(2):213-28. doi: 10.1016/j.physbeh.2009.02.032.

12. The Magic Milestone

1. N. (2019, January 17). *Miscarriage: your questions answered* | Pregnancy articles & support | NCT. NCT (National Childbirth Trust). https://www.nct.org.uk/pregnancy/miscarriage/miscarriage-your-questions-answered
2. Pregnancy test, singular? Who am I kidding? Evelyn took a test an hour for a week. We're still finding those sticks all over the house. We've enough for a full game of Mikado.

14. We're Pregnant

1. Mrayan, L, et al (2019) *Couvade Syndrome Among Jordanian Expectant Fathers.* Am J Mens Health. 2019 Jan-Feb;13(1):1557988318810243. doi: 10.1177/1557988318810243. Epub 2018 Nov 2. PMID: 30387694; PMCID: PMC6771218.

21. Who Are You Again?

1. Belkin, L. (2017, July 22). *Men Gain Weight During Pregnancy*. Motherlode Blog. https://archive.nytimes.com/parenting.blogs.nytimes.-

com/2009/06/02/men-who-swell-with-pregnancy/

23. The Sex

1. Kooper, A, et al (2012, December 12). *Why Do Parents Prefer to Know the Fetal Sex as Part of Invasive Prenatal Testing?* ISRN Obstetrics and Gynecology (Print); Hindawi Publishing Corporation. https://doi.org/10.5402/2012/524537
2. Kearin, M., Pollard, K. R., & Garbett, I. (2014, August 1). *Accuracy of sonographic fetal gender determination: predictions made by sonographers during routine obstetric ultrasound scans.* Australasian Journal of Ultrasound in Medicine; Wiley. https://doi.org/10.1002/j.2205-0140.2014.tb00028.x

25. Pop Culture Lies

1. Lee, N. M., & Saha, S. (2011, June 1). *Nausea and Vomiting of Pregnancy.* Gastroenterology Clinics of North America; Elsevier BV. https://doi.org/10.1016/j.gtc.2011.03.009
2. Mercer, B. (2015). *Premature Rupture of the Membranes.* Protocols for High-Risk Pregnancies: An Evidence Based Approach, 6th ed. Queenan, J. T., Spong, C. Y., and Lockwood, C. J., editors. Pp. 369-382.

35. The Birth, Part 1: You Will Be Too Early

1. Khambalia A, et al (2013). *Predicting date of birth and examining the best time to date a pregnancy.* Int J Gynaecol Obstet. 2013 Nov;123(2):105-9. doi: 10.1016/j.ijgo.2013.05.007. Epub 2013 Aug 6. PMID: 23932061.
2. McFadden, R. (2014, January 17). *Hiroo Onoda, Soldier Who Hid in Jungle for Decades, Dies at 91.* The New York Times. https://www.nytimes.com/2014/01/18/world/asia/hiroo-onoda-imperial-japanese-army-officer-dies-at-91.html

38. The Birth, Part 4: Some Women Like It When...

1. Betran A, et al (2012). *Trends and projections of caesarean section rates: global and regional estimates.* BMJ Glob Health. 2021 Jun;6(6):e005671. doi: 10.1136/bmjgh-2021-005671. PMID: 34130991; PMCID: PMC8208001.

Printed in Great Britain
by Amazon

32709941R00096